CAREERS FOR

NIGHT OWLS

OWLS

& Other Insomniacs

VGM Careers for You Series

CAREERS FOR

NIGHT OWLS

& Other Insomniacs

LOUISE MILLER

SECOND EDITION

VGM Career Books

Chicago   New York   San Francisco   Lisbon   London   Madrid   Mexico City
Milan   New Delhi   San Juan   Seoul   Singapore   Sydney   Toronto

The *McGraw·Hill* Companies

Library of Congress Cataloging-in-Publication Data

Miller, Louise, 1940–
    Careers for night owls & other insomniacs / Louise Miller. — 2nd ed.
        p.   cm. — (VGM careers for you series)
    Includes bibliographical references.
    ISBN 0-07-139034-0 (pbk.)
      1. Vocational guidance.   2. Night work.   3. Night people—Vocational
guidance.   I. Title: Careers for night owls and other insomniacs.   II. Title.
III. Series.

    HF5382 .M52   2002
    331.7'02—dc21   2002069124

1 2 3 4 5 6 7 8 9 0   LBM/LBM   1 0 9 8 7 6 5 4 3 2

ISBN 0-07-139034-0

McGraw-Hill books are available at special quantity discounts to use as premiums and
sales promotions, or for use in corporate training programs. For more information,
please write to the Director of Special Sales, Professional Publishing, McGraw-Hill, Two
Penn Plaza, New York, NY 10121-2298. Or contact your local bookstore.

This book is printed on acid-free paper.

· ·

*To Charles, a dear friend who enhanced
our lives immeasurably with his
generosity, kindness, and understanding
and who will always be remembered*

TM

Contents

Introduction

When I originally conducted research for this book, I was surprised to learn that people perform much the same work at night that other people do during the day. This is good news for people in a variety of circumstances that may prevent them from being employed full-time during the daylight hours. For example, night owls might be stay-at-home moms and dads raising their children during the day and earning income at night or full-time students financing their education without sacrificing time in the classroom. In addition to those who are night owls out of necessity, there are also those who find there are more advantages to working evening hours, including scheduling and keeping doctors', dentists', and other appointments during the day; shopping when there are no crowds; and working during hours when the dress code is more casual.

Currently, the most plentiful work available during the evening hours is in the form of shift work. Indeed, shift work across industries is becoming more and more popular every day. Because of the expanding global market, there is a need for a variety of information, products, and services—and the people to supply them—to be available twenty-four hours a day, every day. However, even though people are working split shifts, graveyard shifts, and downright unpredictable shifts, biology and society are still on the side of people working during the day and sleeping at night.

Increasingly, companies struggle to schedule their employees fairly while balancing productivity and safety concerns. To do so, employers must consider an employee's ability to cope with the pressures of the job, the prevention of accidents and errors occurring on the job, and the preservation of the employee's family life.

Because scheduling can be a sensitive issue for some shift workers who would prefer to work during the daylight hours, a new kind of consulting company has emerged to help companies cope with the problems of scheduling and staff morale. This is just one of several new opportunities available as a result of the increase in the work of night owls.

In fact, some people working the night shift feel so passionately about their jobs that they would work in the same field no matter what the hours. This is often true with people who are involved with life-saving work or the entertainment industry. Others accept shift work as a means to earn a living while they pursue a different job, education, or training in the field of their choice. In fact, all of us may have to consider working nights sooner or later if recent trends continue.

Many of us who work socially and biologically compatible hours take for granted that there are people working afternoon and evening hours to make sure that we are taken care of in a variety of ways. Some of these include:

- Firefighters and police officers
- Actors and directors
- Taxi, bus, and train drivers
- Pilots and flight attendants
- Physicians, veterinarians, and pharmacists
- Hotel managers, concierges, chefs, and housekeepers
- Retail salespersons selling essentials in the middle of the night

Every one of these workers and many others not mentioned here are essential to our peace of mind, health, entertainment, nourishment, and transport. In *Careers for Night Owls & Other Insomniacs,* you'll discover a range of interesting professions requiring different levels of education and training, and you'll meet a variety of people who are earning their livings in the twilight hours. I hope this book serves as a tribute to those workers who keep our world functioning while we sleep, sometimes at great personal sacrifice, and who have shared their stories with us so that others can see if those careers match their dreams and passions. After all, that's what we all look for in our life's work, and I hope you find it in yours!

CHAPTER ONE

Shift Work in a Changing Economy

E ven as the tragic events of September 11, 2001, unfolded before our eyes, the U.S. economy was already tumbling toward a recession. Because of our global economy, what happened here happened all over the world. Many companies went out of business, the stock market plunged, and high-tech dot-coms floundered. Manufacturing jobs were slashed, and companies downsized by the hundreds and thousands worldwide. The boom was over—at least temporarily.

In the process, many companies had to rethink their workforces, including how to best utilize their existing staffs and how to make them productive as well as efficient. Many companies that had expanded capacity and utilized personnel and equipment to the maximum during the boom had to revamp and rethink their resources.

In the third quarter of 2001, employers were asking themselves some tough questions:

- Has demand for our product or service changed?
- If so, how do we reorganize staff and schedules to fit the new market?
- Do we still need to staff on a twenty-four-hour basis?

In good economic times, more employees are needed because the demand for products and services is great. Many of the industries affected by the recession often had different shifts during those good times. These industries may now be looking to change

I

their schedules to better reflect demand. And no matter how good or bad the economy is, a well-planned schedule is important, and shift work is still necessary for many jobs.

For example, law enforcement and health care personnel, factory workers, firefighters, transportation workers, and military personnel have traditionally functioned with shift work. Nonstandard work schedules vary widely:

- Some companies have three shifts, running twenty-four hours a day, seven days a week; employees working the overnight shift are said to work the graveyard shift.
- Others have split shifts, working mornings and evenings with afternoons off.
- Still others have rotating shifts, with employees working a few days during the day and a few at night.

But as the global economy fluctuates, employers are thinking of building flexibility into their schedules so that a smooth transition can be made as economic circumstances change. Managing shift work in a downtime is cost effective but requires planning and communication with employees.

The Need for Shift Work

Since our world runs on a twenty-four-hour basis, we need people to fulfill certain needs on that same basis. The obvious shift-work jobs have already been mentioned, but let's see more specifically how night-shift workers help us.

We may need medicine or gas for the car in the middle of the night. All-night pharmacies and gas stations are there for us. Or maybe we are hungry and would like to find a restaurant or grocery store open at midnight. Many overnight coffeehouses and convenience stores fill the bill.

Getting to the hospital often requires the use of an ambulance, and not having medical caretakers ready to help is unimaginable.

Doctors, nurses, paramedics, and technicians will be there to help. Emergency room veterinarians are also available for the pet that becomes sick in the middle of the night. Even getting home from a late-night party might be difficult without buses, trains, or cabs. And goods and passengers would not be transported from place to place without truck drivers, pilots, and flight attendants who work shifts.

Without firefighters and police officers, we would not feel secure at night, and emergency snow crews make sure we get to work in the morning. The newspaper is waiting for us when we wake up, thanks to the overnight crew of reporters, photographers, writers, editors, printers, and delivery people who work the graveyard shift. And if we're insomniacs and want the news at 3 A.M., the all-night cable network news crew is busy at work.

After a long nine-to-five day at work, we might want to take in a play or go to a club, bar, or concert to relax. Actors, directors, dancers, musicians, singers, waiters, bartenders, cooks, hosts, and hostesses are there to see that we have a good time. And when we travel, there's nothing more comforting than to get to our hotel room, have a good meal, and get a good night's sleep. There to make sure that our stay is as comfortable and clean as possible, no matter when we arrive, are the desk clerk, housekeeping staff, room service personnel, and, of course, behind it all, the hotel manager.

How Do We Prepare for Change?

When the economy shifts, so too might schedules for a variety of jobs. Therefore, we will take a look at the advantages and disadvantages of working nonstandard hours because options may become available in a changing economy that we haven't had before. And we should all, employers and employees alike, be flexible enough to adjust to "shifting" circumstances.

Many employees like to work nonstandard hours, especially if they have a regular schedule that doesn't rotate. They work the same time every day and adjust their personal lives around those hours. Many enjoy the fact that they can schedule doctors' and dentists' appointments, go shopping, and receive services when everyone else is at work. Often the work atmosphere is more relaxed, and the phone doesn't ring as much at night.

However, in any transitional process, employer and employee have to remember that people have social and psychological needs. And although some employees may like some of the conveniences of working nonstandard hours, some adverse consequences can occur when they work against the clock. That is because we all have a built-in clock that corresponds to our circadian rhythms. The word *circadian* comes from two Latin words: *circa* (about) and *dia* (day). These rhythms are connected to the earth's twenty-four-hour turn on its axis that tells us to be awake during the day and to sleep at night. Since shift work disturbs these natural rhythms, employer and employee must seriously consider the implications when making out the work schedule.

The Sleep/Wake Cycle

Circadian rhythms occur periodically throughout the day, and more and more of them are being recognized. The most common to date is the sleep/wake cycle, but body temperature and maybe even bone length play a role in our natural rhythms.

Both employers and employees have to take not only these physical needs into consideration when scheduling shifts, but also social, family, and safety needs. Employees have to work out their new schedules with their families and friends and elicit their support. Consultants may be available to help families adjust to the stress of the new schedule. Consulting companies are also now available to help employers analyze their needs and communicate with their employees to help solve their problems.

Working the night shift can play havoc with the natural circadian rhythms; this condition is often called shift lag. It is comparable to jet lag—the phenomenon we experience when we travel through different time zones in a comparatively short period of time. Some of the symptoms include increased irritability and sensitivity, defensive and contrary behavior, forgetfulness, and moodiness.

Body temperature is a good indicator of how your rhythm actually works. As the temperature drops, so does your energy level. Body temperature typically lowers between 11:00 P.M. and midnight and continues to drop until about 4:30 A.M. The body is at its lowest level at 3:00 A.M. when it is literally resetting its clock. The temperature begins to rise again at around 6:00 A.M. When a worker has a constantly changing shift, it is difficult to change the rhythm of the body temperature.

Also contributing to night shift workers' problems is that they often do not eat the right food during the shift and may also become dehydrated. To keep awake, they often drink too much caffeine in coffee or soft drinks. All this can lead to fatigue, interrupted sleep, stomach problems, and low energy. More mistakes can also occur under these circumstances.

Coping Mechanisms

Since so many problems facing the shift worker revolve around the sleep/wake cycle, which is closely related to body temperature, some studies indicate that bright light therapy upon waking at night and total darkness when sleeping during the day can help shift workers make the transition. Other tips to assure a quality sleep include quiet, temperature and humidity control, a comfortable bed, and earplugs. Moderate exercise, good nutrition, and plenty of liquids to reduce dehydration will also help in getting a good day's sleep.

If your job is particularly stressful, you will have to analyze your lifestyle and try to make healthy changes. You and your family will have to prioritize duties and responsibilities, and all family members should be aware of your schedule. Certain changes may have to be made for everyone to feel important and not neglected. This is especially true if the shift worker is not available for family celebrations, such as birthdays, graduations, school plays, and holidays. In those cases, compromises may have to be made, such as celebrating Thanksgiving on the following Friday or Saturday.

Working with the Employer

Employers who have to adjust schedules to the changing economy may seek the services of consulting companies that are set up to help. These companies discuss problems with management and the affected employees. They figure out costs and training needs, review policies and procedures, and make recommendations. When everyone is involved, the plan is usually implemented with fewer difficulties. Some companies even provide spreadsheet software to facilitate setting up new schedules.

How You Can Prepare for Shift Work

Some jobs may always belong to the traditional economy; others will become a part of the new one. If you are called on to work nonstandard hours, you may want to talk to other people who have experience with shift work. Discuss the pros and cons with them and why they like or dislike it. Find out how they juggle the work schedule with family and friends, when they celebrate holidays and family affairs. Research industries to see which ones always need to use shift workers and which may need them in the future. The Internet is a good source of information as you conduct your research. Just click the keywords *night shift* and you will be referred to links that will help you assess your possible place in the changing workplace. You may also want to consult the *Occupational Outlook Handbook,* published by the Bureau of Labor Statistics of the U.S. Department of Labor, either online or at your local library. (The salaries in this book are taken from the bureau's statistics.) Then pursue the career that you really want. We will present some of the possibilities in the following chapters.

For Further Information

American College of Emergency Physicians
1125 Executive Circle
Irving, TX 75037

Shiftwork Solutions LLC
950 Northgate Drive, Suite 309
San Rafael, CA 94903

Plain English About Shiftwork. National Institute for
Occupational Safety and Health (DHHS), No. 97-145.

CHAPTER TWO

On Wings and Wheels

All of us have to get somewhere at some time. If you need to be somewhere else in the morning, chances are that you will be traveling at night. Wings and wheels get you wherever you have to go with the aid of pilots, flight attendants, cab and bus drivers, engineers, and conductors. If goods have to be shipped across country, truck drivers will be driving through the night. Cab and bus drivers work the city streets when most of us are sleeping.

Night-Owl Careers on Wings

The airline industry was severely affected by the events of September 11 and the recession of 2001. Thousands of employees were laid off and flights were canceled for lack of passengers. Increased security at the airports, although necessary, also put off the traveling public because of the delays it entailed. But primarily affecting the flying public was the horrifying image of planes attacking the World Trade Center towers in New York. As with any personal loss or tragedy, time will tell how long the public will take to feel secure in the air again, but it would be premature to say that the industry will not recover. When that recovery occurs, more jobs will again become available, and more flights will take place overnight. Even now, the airlines need specific personnel:

- A captain, the chief pilot, who is responsible for all safety aspects of the flight

- The copilot, who is second in command to the captain
- The second officer or flight engineer, who sees to the mechanical and electronic functions of the aircraft
- The flight attendants, who oversee the safety and comfort of the passengers
- A flight dispatcher, who determines when the aircraft may take off and land and monitors the flight to its final destination

Pilots, Flight Engineers, and Captains

The top job in a commercial airline is the captain, but you don't get to be captain overnight—it takes years of service as a pilot after years of thorough training and certification.

In order to become a pilot, you first have to get a commercial pilot's license and an instrument rating from the Federal Aviation Administration (FAA). You have to be at least eighteen years old and have flown at least 250 hours. You will have to pass a thorough physical examination, have 20/20 vision, and pass a written examination. Then FAA examiners test your flying ability. The physical and flying exams have to be repeated periodically in order to keep your license valid.

To become a flight engineer for an airline, you have to pass further FAA exams. And to become a captain, you have to have an airline transport pilot's license. For this, you have to be at least twenty-three years old and have flown at least fifteen hundred hours. You can get an FAA rating for bad-weather, night, and instrument flying with further testing and flying demonstrations.

Many people start flying during military training, while others learn at colleges, universities, or private flying schools. About six hundred flying schools around the country have already received FAA certification. You will have to have at least a high school diploma to become a commercial pilot, but more and more airlines are looking for college graduates for these positions.

Legally, airline pilots may not fly more than one hundred hours per month or more than a thousand hours a year. They usually fly about seventy-five hours each month and can spend the same amount of time on nonflying responsibilities. Some of these duties, especially for charter pilots, include keeping records, loading cargo, scheduling flights, or working on maintenance projects. Since commercial airlines operate twenty-four hours a day, seven days a week, pilots are often required to work nonstandard hours. Since they often experience jet lag, the FAA demands that airlines require pilots to have at least eight hours of uninterrupted rest in the twenty-four hours before they finish their flight duties.

In 2000, about 117,000 jobs were held by aircraft pilots and flight engineers. The average annual salary for commercial pilots, copilots, and flight engineers in 2000 was $110,940. Competition for these jobs is always high and may be even more intense in difficult economic times.

Pilots are also needed to fly helicopters, however, and to dust crops, test aircraft, teach flying, help with fire fighting efforts, and assist in evacuations in emergencies and disasters. These pilots are often required to work irregular hours but may return home at night.

Flight Attendants

The flight attendants work in the cabin of the plane. Their work begins even before the passengers board. That's when they prepare the cabin for flight by seeing that food and beverage supplies, reading materials, pillows, blankets, and first-aid kits are where they belong. They also receive instructions from the pilot regarding emergencies, weather conditions, and duration of the flight. When passengers board the plane, the attendants check tickets and assist passengers with storing luggage, locating their seats, and caring for special needs.

Since the most important function of the flight attendants is the passengers' safety, they also are required to give visual instructions on what passengers should do in an emergency. If one actually occurs, they make sure that the emergency exits are open and that the chutes are inflated for evacuation. They also make sure that passengers' seat belts are fastened and that their seats are upright before takeoff and during landing.

During the flight, attendants serve food and beverages, help passengers who need special care, and administer first aid as needed. When the plane lands, they help passengers out of the plane. After the flight, they often have to write reports, collect items left behind, and generally check the condition of the cabin.

If you want to become a flight attendant, you have to be at least eighteen to twenty-one years old for most commercial airlines and a high school graduate. A college education is a plus. Airlines provide training for flight attendants that includes emergency procedures, giving first aid, and how to deal with unruly passengers or hijackers. If you decide to work for an international airline, you will also have to speak the pertinent foreign language fluently. Your health and communication skills have to be excellent as an attendant because you will be on your feet most of the time, the work can be stressful, and you always have to be congenial with the passengers.

You also have to be prepared for an irregular schedule, often working holidays, weekends, and overnight. You will probably fly eighty hours a month on the average and be on the ground the same number of hours. If you must stay overnight in another city, the airline usually provides a hotel room and meals.

In 2000, the average annual salary for flight attendants was $38,820, with the lowest 10 percent earning under $18,090 and the top 10 percent more than $83,630. Some flight attendants are paid more for night flights. They often get eleven days off a month as well as free fares for themselves and their immediate families and discounts on other airlines. Flight attendants can move up to become senior flight attendants or flight attendant instructors, customer service directors, or recruiting representatives.

Flight Dispatchers

Flight dispatchers work with the pilot to provide a flight plan with maximum cargo and passengers at the lowest cost. In order to do this, the dispatcher has to evaluate weather conditions in the air and at the destination city, judge how much fuel is needed, and analyze traffic patterns. The dispatcher has to be aware of all dispatched flights and report to both the pilot and personnel on the ground. They have to know all routes and facilities at the airport and the takeoff and landing capabilities of all appropriate aircraft.

Air Traffic Controllers

Without air traffic controllers, no flight would be safe—day or night. These highly trained specialists help to determine the arrivals and departures of all civilian and military flights. As such, they are essential for national defense and civilian safety. Controllers can be employed by the FAA, the Department of Defense (DOD), local or state governments, or private airlines.

Air traffic controllers have various responsibilities:

- **Terminal area air traffic controllers** supply the pilot with weather conditions, takeoff and landing clearance, and information about other aircraft approaching, leaving, or flying through the airport. They use radio, radar, or visual observation to make sure that planes are a safe distance from each other in the air and on the runway. Radar can detect planes at least forty miles from the airport, which will allow for a safe landing and departure.
- **En route controllers** are FAA employees who work in centers located throughout the country. They take the aircraft, operating according to instrument flight rules, through the airspace from airport to airport. They transmit weather and traffic information to the pilots, and pilots transmit their positions along the way. They can also ask for a change in route or altitude during the flight.
- **Flight services specialists** are responsible for preflight information about weather and general airport conditions. They send the pilot's flight plan to the air traffic controller and to the flight service station at the destination airport.

To become an air traffic control specialist, you start as a trainee selected through the Federal Civil Service system. You have to take a written test to see if you have the ability to do the work. Generally, you must have three years of work experience or four years of college. You then move on to the FAA Academy in Oklahoma City, where you continue your training and testing. Then you receive on-the-job training. Qualities recommended for an air traffic controller include having good communication skills and an ability to make quick decisions.

The work itself is demanding and requires rotating shift work because air travel is available twenty-four hours a day, year-round. The shifts vary depending on the individual facility's workload and traffic patterns. Those controllers working for the FAA, the DOD, or the Department of Transportation (DOT) receive more pay when they work Sundays, holidays, or nights.

The most recent salary figures for air traffic controllers show median annual wages at $64,880, with the lowest 10 percent earning less than $36,640 and the top earning $87,210.

Other Shift Workers at the Airport

At the airport, you will also find ticket agents who figure out fares, write tickets, check in baggage, and answer questions about departures and arrivals. The skycaps help you with your luggage, and food service employees make sure you have something to eat during the flight. Baggage handlers make sure you get your luggage after the flight.

All these careers have shift work built in. They include rotating shifts and graveyard shifts. So if you're a night owl who'd like to be involved in the travel industry, there are ample opportunities for you to choose from.

Profile of a Flight Attendant

Vicki McIntyre-Brezinski has worked every shift the airline has to offer. Irregular hours are not strange to Vicki, whose father was a pilot with different schedules each week and each month. Vicki grew up with a positive image of these crazy hours because, after all, her father's job provided the family with food and clothing—and travel privileges. Life was more casual, especially at mealtime, when her father was working. However, mealtime was much more formal when he was home because it was a rare event.

Holidays were often celebrated later in her home than the actual date. So after her friends had already played with their toys for a few days after Christmas, she was just receiving her new ones. She learned to like this system and realized that she did not identify with people who lived for the weekend and had to celebrate holidays strictly on that day. In other words, she learned flexibility at an early age.

Vicki did not consciously pursue an alternate work style, but she certainly did not resist it. She was always encouraged to try everything, even though it might be different from what everyone else did. Actually, Vicki started out as a musician—a drummer. This was unusual for a female, but she played in combos in high school and college, loved the applause, and became addicted to the night life.

She was playing with a band in Hawaii but had to return home for treatment of a kidney ailment. During that time, the band broke up. She did not want to sign up with an agent, but she did want some job security. The airline offered security and a possible chance to return to Hawaii.

She was hired as a clerk in dispatch with honest-to-goodness rotating shift work. Vicki was working one week of mornings, one week of nights, and one week of afternoons, on six days, off two. The dispatchers had done it for years, and she fell in love with it. She loved not having to fight rush-hour traffic and crowded stores.

After a year as a clerk, Vicki was hired as a flight attendant. Although it was probably more her parents' dream than her own, she thought that she might, as a flight attendant, get to Hawaii to reestablish her musical connections.

As luck would have it, the airline wanted to use both her skills and allowed her to participate in musical road shows on behalf of the airline to raise morale for other employees. This experience helped Vicki realize that she had made a successful transition from the music world to a profession that offered more security and benefits than being a musician.

Vicki had the opportunity to work nine to five when she was transferred to a ground supervisor position with regular hours. Within months, she was miserable. She hated the rush-hour traffic, the crowded stores, and the repetition of the work—seeing the same faces every day. Although she did it for a year, she cried every day during the last three months of the job.

Vicki seems to be made for the night shift. As an international flight attendant, she flies mostly at night, and that makes her very happy because passengers are simply less demanding when they are asleep! But the attraction to night work for Vicki is still the diversity of the changing schedules, coworkers, and customers.

Even Vicki admits that after so many years, the duties become routine. Therefore, she has to face the challenge of not slipping into complacency, especially with the passengers. She does that with a large dose of empathy—she puts herself in the passengers' shoes and tries to make them as comfortable as she would like to be. Also, her sense of humor allows her the freedom to entertain a built-in audience and the knowledge that she will never see the disagreeable ones again.

The only frustration that Vicki has working her strange and rotating hours is trying to function in a society that thinks nine to five is normal. For instance, she finds it hard to get a doctor's or dentist's appointment when she doesn't know her schedule for the following month until the twentieth of the previous month. Sometimes the only appointment available is for 10 A.M. when she has just arrived home at 5 A.M. When she has a series of trips, it's difficult to find grocery stores, cleaners, and department stores to match her weird hours, even though there are more twenty-four-hour facilities available now than ever before. It is also difficult trying to manage a social life with people who work "straight" hours, including having all weekends off.

After many years as a single woman, Vicki married a television editor who also has very irregular work hours. Luckily they understand the unpredictability of each other's jobs. But in the process, Vicki had to deal with a family who initially couldn't understand why she might not be around for the scheduled holidays.

Jet lag and time zone changes are also challenges for international travelers. Vicki thinks that you really never overcome it; you just learn to adjust to it. You also can't possibly try to combine regular and irregular hours to keep up a social life. You will only become dysfunctional from exhaustion. It takes Vicki about a day or two to adjust to being home after a long trip. Luckily her family gives her the time and space to recuperate in her own way.

Even though she does experience some hardships with her alternate lifestyle, Vicki wouldn't change it. But some things definitely make it easier for her. For example, she cites twenty-four-hour shopping facilities, cellular phones, and increasing acceptance of five-to-nine schedules by those who work more traditional hours.

Vicki thinks that with the growing population in this country, coupled with the advent of the communications superhighway and high-tech advances, many companies will have more in-home workers. Alternative work hours will have to overlap somewhat with traditional ones, and if these "abnormal" work shifts become more "normal," additional pay will not be offered for the graveyard shift. Until then, Vicki is very happy with her odd hours. She feels that those who work alternate hours are independent, flexible, and adventurous. And Vicki seems to fit that glove very well.

Night-Owl Careers on Wheels

Back on land, we need bus, cab, and truck drivers, as well as railroad workers, to move us around to hotels, offices, and restaurants and to deliver food, beverages, medicine, furniture, and all manner of goods that we need for our daily lives. Night work is necessary for all these jobs.

Commercial Drivers and Truckers

Long-haul truck drivers can be away from home overnight, or they might be driving all week, with stops for food, rest, refueling, and unloading. Sometimes they have a regular run; other times, dispatchers inform them where to go next. At the end of the run, the drivers have to fill in reports on the trip, including details of any accidents. This is required by the Department of Transportation (DOT).

The DOT regulates all trucking companies that deal in interstate commerce regarding work hours for the drivers. Individual states also have standards for truck drivers, including licensing procedures. Bus and truck drivers must adhere to the Motor Vehicle Safety Act of 1986. If you drive a vehicle with sixteen or more passengers, for example, you must have a Commercial Driver's License (CDL). A truck driver who drives a truck with a twenty-six-thousand-pound capacity also has to have a CDL.

Generally speaking, drivers must be at least twenty-one years old and in good physical condition, including hearing and vision. You can make a good living as a long-distance truck driver if you know the rules of the road and are willing to drive at night and work alone for long stretches at a time.

Bus Drivers

Some bus drivers work for private companies and transport people within a state or across country. Municipal bus drivers provide transportation for those who are out on the town, including all those workers who have the graveyard shift.

Their responsibilities include collecting fares and assisting customers with routes and transfers. The primary responsibility, however, is to transport passengers safely from place to place. They may work irregular hours, including holidays, weekends, and evenings.

Bus drivers usually receive from two to eight weeks of training, where they learn rules and regulations, fare structure, and how to read schedules. They also get hands-on training driving the bus, including how to deal courteously with passengers. Since pay and benefits vary widely from city to city and company to company, you should check these out on an individual basis.

Railroad Workers

You may also decide to work for a railroad if you are interested in transportation. You wouldn't be alone: in the year 2000, more than 115,000 people were working for the railroads in this country. Trains transport people and freight, just as airplanes do, and specific jobs are available on the railroads: engineers, switchers, yardmasters, brake operators, conductors, and train dispatchers.

Engineers run the trains, check them before and after the trip, monitor all the gauges during the trip, and keep in radio contact with traffic control centers about stops, starts, or delays.

Switchers operate the switches that move trains from track to track, keeping in radio contact with the yard engineer. Switchers can become yardmasters, who monitor panels and activate the switches and lights. Brake operators are part of the crew on freight trains. They inspect the train and make sure that it is on the right track. Passenger conductors collect tickets, assist passengers, and see to the safety of passengers in an emergency. Dispatchers keep track of the movement of the trains, monitor the display panel, and transmit information to the engineer by radio.

It is rare for engineers, conductors, and brake operators to have regular hours. Their names go on an assignment board, and when they reach the designated number of miles, the next person on the board takes the run. Those with little seniority are on call twenty-four hours.

You can get on-the-job training as a railroad worker. To become an engineer, you must be at least twenty-one, have a high school diploma or equivalent, be in good physical condition, and complete the training course. Sometimes you can become an engineer after being a brake operator or yard laborer.

Your salary will vary from company to company, but you must be certified and licensed by the Federal Railroad Administration.

However, you should keep in mind that this job, as well as that of bus driver and flight attendant, was recently listed as a high-stress profession by the National Institute for Occupational Safety and Health.

Cab Drivers

All jobs that deal with the public are generally considered to be high-stress positions, including driving a cab. And although you don't need any special education to be a driver, you do need good communication skills in English; knowledge of the city you are driving in, along with map-reading skills; the ability to get along with a great variety of people, sometimes from all over the world; and, of course, excellent driving skills. All these skills combine to make you a good cab driver.

You will also have to go through a brief training period, pass a written test, and have a valid chauffeur's license. Since cabs run twenty-four hours a day, every day of the year, you may get the graveyard shift.

Many cities issue guidelines for consumers so they know what to expect from cab companies and drivers. The guidelines often remind passengers to accept rides only from licensed cabs and outline where the drivers are allowed to go and what you should expect as far as fares are concerned.

The brochure also may caution the consumer to note license numbers, pictures of the cab drivers that are prominently displayed, and the medallion numbers. These identifications are important in case you leave something in the cab or have a complaint about the driver. And although there are always a million horror stories about driving in any big city, we simply can't get along without cab drivers!

Profile of a Cab Driver

Rick Springer has been a cab driver in Chicago for several years. He knows about the stresses and real fears related to the job. For six years before he started driving, he was an inside salesperson for both veterinary medicine and for machine tools for heavy industry.

When the economy began to sag, he was laid off and was out of work for about one and a half years. He worked part-time as a carpet cleaner until the company lost its biggest account, and that was the end of that. At that point, Rick was fifty-five years old with very few marketable skills. But his back was up against a very hard wall, and he had to make some difficult decisions.

One of his friends, who had been a cab driver for several years, urged him to get his chauffeur's license and become a cab driver. As much as he needed a job, Rick didn't want anything to do with driving a cab—because he hated cab drivers. He thought they were terrible drivers, had bad attitudes toward other drivers, and didn't know how to get around the city. He also had some fears about being robbed or shot as a cab driver in a big city.

As a longtime resident of Chicago, however, Rick felt that he really knew his way around, and he also knew he was a very good driver. Since he had, at one point in his life, delivered pizzas at night, he knew how to make a living with his driving skills. Still, he had his doubts, mainly because nighttime drivers are very vulnerable to robbery or worse.

But his money was dwindling, and his friend kept pushing, so Rick decided to pay the $25 application fee for classes to earn a chauffeur's license. Along with the $25, he had to have a valid driver's license and be free and clear of traffic tickets.

He then took a three-day course that covered a lot of ground. Rick had to learn where hospitals, hotels, police stations, major tourist attractions, universities, and sports facilities are located. He had to study street guides and maps of the city; he had to know about the best routes to get from here to there; and he had to know the rules of the road and the laws pertaining to driving a cab. These included regulations for limiting the number of passengers allowed in the cab, jumping in front of other cabs in a pickup line, and picking up all passengers regardless of appearance or destination.

Oral communications were tested in class, and a written test was given at the end of the course. Although you don't have to fulfill any educational requirements to drive a cab, you do have to be able to communicate in English.

Rick passed the test the first time and then had to interview with a cab company—even though he still didn't want to be a cab driver. Again, his friend pushed him to interview. He did, but he failed an oral test that was a major part of the interview. Rick went back to the books and passed the next time. He finally took the plunge and decided to take the night shift, even though he still had some doubts about his decision.

He was still worried about security, but he was also afraid that his first passenger would want to go to some exotic location that he had never heard of. He was afraid that he wouldn't know the best routes and that he would disappoint his customer.

With a little time, though, Rick began to have fun on the job. Now he works four nights a week: Monday, Wednesday, Friday, and Saturday. On weeknights, he works from 5:00 P.M. to about 1:30 A.M. On weekends, he works from 5:00 P.M. to 2:00 A.M., when the bars close. For most of his life, Rick was a "day" person, working from nine to five. The adjustment took a few months, but now he is almost addicted to the job and the hours.

Rick loves the independence of the job, knowing that he can stop and start when he wants. He also loves to drive and meet people from all over the world and has gained new appreciation for the beauty and cleanliness of Chicago from his passengers.

Another bonus for him is that he earns his pay in cash directly and immediately. But because of this, he has to keep exact tax records because no deductions are taken from his pay. If he didn't have hospitalization coverage through the Veterans Administration, he would also be responsible for his own health care expenses.

Some of the fun for Rick also has to do with what he calls the "hunt." He is on the prowl for customers, and other cab drivers are the enemy. He loves to get those passengers into his cab and thinks it a great challenge to get them safely to their destinations in the shortest possible time. Rick also loves the compliments he gets for finding unusual routes and for his good driving.

Although Rick enjoys having his weekdays free for fishing, golf, and museum hopping, sometimes he feels isolated and lonely because his friends are working during the day. Since he works on Friday and Saturday nights, his social life has also suffered because most of his friends are winding down their weekends on Sunday afternoon when he's just getting up.

On the other hand, it is very easy to get appointments with doctors and dentists, and shopping during the day is a pleasure. When he goes fishing during the week, Rick can fish on calm waters with very few other people to distract him or the fish.

To be a good cab driver, Rick thinks that you have to be a good driver first. You also have to have good vision and like people. It doesn't hurt to have a good radio in your cab as well as a beaded seat to relieve muscle tension and fatigue. He thinks that everybody should drive a cab for a while.

Is a Career in Transportation Right for You?

Careers in transportation offer a wide variety of work for people with different educational and career backgrounds. You can set your goals, choose your mode of transportation, and then set your course. You can wing it or wheel it, but you must at least go for it.

Since many jobs in transportation entail working with the public and doing shift work, you might ask yourself some questions before you finally decide to take the plunge. For example, flight attendants, bus and cab drivers, and train conductors deal directly with people as part of the job. A pleasant personality, a sense of humor, and a true feeling for other people's comfort and security are important qualities for these jobs. Pilots, train engineers, and air traffic control specialists work under the pressures of passenger security, weather conditions, and sometimes life-and-death decision making.

As you try to decide on a career in transportation, you might look into your personal life experiences to see if this is the place for you. Let's see, for example, how you might answer the following questions:

1. If there is a family crisis, are you able to keep a level head when everyone else is in turmoil?
2. Do you like to participate in social activities or clubs because you genuinely like to be with people?
3. Do you like to travel and meet people who are different from you—speak a different language, come from another country, go to a different church?
4. If you ever worked in a store, did you go out of your way to make sure that the customers were taken care of and satisfied with their purchases?
5. Are you flexible—could you be happy with a schedule that changed every day?
6. Are you independent—can you make decisions without needing people to tell you what to do?
7. Are you able to laugh at yourself if you've made a mistake and learn from it?
8. Are you a responsible driver with a clean driving record?
9. Can you communicate well with other people? In English? In any other language?
10. Can you do a job or complete a project without being constantly supervised?

If you answered yes to all of the questions, you're well on your way to a career in some phase of transportation. Now you just have to find your niche and pursue your goal.

For Further Information

You may obtain a variety of publications through these organizations, and more information is available online at the websites.

Air Line Pilots Association
535 Herndon Parkway
Herndon, VA 22070
www.alpa.org

Air Traffic Control Association
2300 Clarendon Boulevard, Suite 711
Arlington, VA 22201
www.atca.org

Air Transport Association of America
1301 Pennsylvania Avenue NW, Suite 1110
Washington, DC 20006
www.airlines.org

American Bus Association
1100 New York Avenue NW, Suite 1050
Washington, DC 20005
www.buses.org

American Public Transportation Association
1666 K Street NW, Suite 1100
Washington, DC 20006
www.apta.org

American Trucking Associations
2200 Mill Road
Alexandria, VA 22314
www.truckline.com/infocenter

Association of American Railroads
50 F Street NW
Washington, DC 20001
www.aar.org

Brotherhood of Locomotive Engineers
Standard Building
1370 Ontario Street, Mezzanine
Cleveland, OH 44113
www.ble.org

Federal Aviation Association (FAA) Headquarters
    Office/AHR-15
800 Independence Avenue SW
Washington, DC 20591
www.faa.gov

Helicopter Association International
1619 Duke Street
Alexandria, VA 22314
www.rotor.com

National Highway Traffic Safety Administration
U.S. Department of Transportation
NTS-22
400 Seventh Street SW
Washington, DC 20590
www.nhtsa.dot.gov

CHAPTER THREE

Hotels, Restaurants, and Bars

Hospitality at Its Best

All industries were affected adversely by the terrorist attacks of September 11 and the recession—none more seriously than the hospitality industry. With so many people out of work, many families cannot afford to eat out, and clubs and bars also suffer from lack of customers. Fewer tourists and business travelers fill the hotel rooms since people are hesitant to travel, and corporate budgets have been reduced. However, this economy will eventually turn the corner, and the hospitality industry will get back to normal.

And what does the word *hospitality* conjure up for the weary worker and traveler? Usually it means a clean room, comfortable bed, room service, congenial employees, chocolates on the pillow of the turned-down bed, soaps and shampoos in the bathroom ready for our use, and the luxury of having breakfast in bed, a friendly drink at the bar, and a good meal.

Hospitality also means people who help us with our luggage and arrange for tickets and restaurant reservations. It involves still others who know how to direct us around a new town to see the best sights or get to our business meeting.

These are the people in the hotel and restaurant field, better known as the hospitality industry. The one thing all these people have in common is the goal of pleasing the customer. Whether you decide to be a bellhop or the manager of a huge hotel, serving the guest is your primary goal.

Because this is a worldwide industry, your job possibilities are truly global. Even if you work in the United States, you will meet people from all over the world. Each day can be a new adventure because each day may bring new guests from anywhere in the world whose needs must be met. The skills you learn in the United States can also be easily transferred to hotels and restaurants in other countries.

Hospitality Careers for Night Owls

Let's take a look at some of the jobs available in hotels and motels. You could become a front-desk clerk, chef, food server, bartender, or housekeeper. You could work your way up to assistant general manager and finally manager. And this is just a partial list of possible jobs for you to explore.

Getting Started

There are several ways to begin a career in hotels and motels. Since hours are flexible, you may be able to get a part-time job with a hotel while you are still in high school or college. Some high schools and many junior colleges, four-year colleges, and universities now offer courses in hotel management, which provide an excellent way to break into the field. Although it is still possible to start at the bottom of the ladder and work your way up to top management, more and more hotels and motels are requiring degrees and specialized training in order to advance. The more training and education you receive along the way, the more valuable you are to the organization.

The industry does, however, take pride in providing thorough on-the-job training and promotion from within. Many businesses offer opportunities for continuing education and flexible hours. Since so many jobs operate on a twenty-one-shift week instead of the normal five, schedules can often be arranged to comply with the needs of mothers, students, or senior citizens.

If you work for a hotel or motel chain, one of the benefits of employment is that you may be able to relocate to other cities in this country or in the world. Competitive salaries, life insurance, savings plans, and health insurance are standard benefits in most hotels. Some also provide free meals, laundry or dry cleaning, paid vacations, and training programs.

······················

Hotel Clerks

If you have a lot of patience and want to help everyone who stays at the hotel, you may want to consider the front-desk position. These employees check the guests in and out, assign rooms, assist guests in getting around town, and often help the concierge in making reservations. They answer questions guests have about the hotel and its services, the time it takes to get to the airport, shopping opportunities, and the best sights and restaurants in town.

Many hotels will train you to be a desk clerk if you demonstrate certain qualities. Clerks have to be flexible, courteous, and patient because a good personality and knowledge are extremely important in ensuring that the guests have a pleasant stay, making it more likely that they will return.

Some responsibilities of desk clerks have changed because of the new technology. For example, automated check-in and check-out processes are now available at larger hotels. In those cases, the desk clerk may take on other responsibilities.

In 2000, approximately 177,000 people were employed as front-desk clerks, and, since this job often required flexible schedules, night owls should be quite comfortable in this position. Desk clerk positions are not only dependent on the general economy but also by those seasons when most tourists come to town.

······················

Housekeepers

No matter how long we stay in a hotel, probably the most important element in our comfort is our room. All the great food in the world can't make up for a room that is not clean or well maintained. We love clean sheets and towels; shampoo, soaps, and tissues in the bathroom; newly vacuumed carpets; and polished furniture and mirrors. We like to think that no one else has ever been there before us. For all this cleanliness and comfort, we have the housekeeping staff to thank.

In hotels, housekeeping is always one of the largest departments—in larger hotels, there may be several hundred employees. Both staff members and executives usually work longer hours during tourist season, when everybody may be on call.

The room attendants, laundry personnel, linen-room workers, and floor supervisors are all part of that staff, with the executive housekeeper as the overall supervisor. It has been customary for this position to be filled by a senior staff member. However, there are now college courses and certification programs that prepare you for this management position.

Education and Training

Room attendants and laundry personnel generally do not need specific education or training. Most learn their skills on the job. However, to advance to an executive position, you will need to have specific education, training, and skills. Recommended college courses are sociology, psychology, economics, communications, and budgeting. Accounting and computer classes are always helpful. You will need good organizational, communications, and motivational skills.

Job prospects are good, especially if you have education and experience. Since the executive housekeeper position is at the top of the housekeeping department, you could advance to become assistant manager and then general manager.

Hotel Managers

The top position in most hotels and motels is the general manager. These managers are in charge of the overall operation of the hotel, including preparing the budget, setting quality standards for all departments, and following the policies of the owner or hotel chain executive. Many of the larger hotels have assistant general managers for each of the various departments.

Like other lodging industry employees, managers work odd hours: evenings, nights, weekends, and holidays, with particularly long hours during conventions or peak tourist seasons. Managers can work for a corporation or own their own establishments.

Education and Training

As in all other hotel positions, training and education are important because the industry is becoming more and more professional. Managers, in particular, must have college degrees. A liberal arts degree is acceptable if you also have some hotel or restaurant management experience. However, you can now get a bachelor's degree in hotel management. Courses include accounting, marketing, housekeeping, and data processing. Working a hotel job during breaks or after school in conjunction with your degree gives you a better chance at landing a managerial position.

It still is possible, in some hotels, to get on-the-job training by working in every department until you learn all aspects of the hotel's operations. You also may be required to relocate to other hotels or motels in the chain. Certification, including course work, from the American Hotel & Lodging Association can land you a management position in conjunction with this training.

Earnings

The median salary for hotel managers was $30,770 in 2000. Salaries vary depending on the size of the hotel and the extent of the responsibilities. Benefits are usually good, and bonuses can be earned up to 25 percent of base salary.

Profile of a Former Hotel Manager

Dean Kelley indirectly got his current job in a bank because of his background in the hotel business. He served first as concierge for the bank, after many years of working for various hotels and motels—and that included working nights and being on call twenty-four hours a day.

When Dean was a sophomore in college, he worked part-time at a local hotel. This job included maintenance and repair work, with hours from either 3 to 11 P.M. or 4 P.M. to midnight. He was working on his B.A. in business, but there were no hospitality courses offered at that time. He was at a point in his life, though, when he was wondering what he was going to do for a living.

The hotel business seemed to offer good opportunities for quick advancement and good salaries. So, with a combination of his experience at the hotel and his college education, he thought he could rapidly become an assistant manager of a small property.

That's exactly what happened. After graduating from college, he became assistant manager for a Red Roof Inn in Grand Rapids, Michigan. He started out learning how to work the night audit, which included front-desk work and balancing the books.

After that, he went to Atlanta, Georgia, to the company's general manager training school, where he learned operational procedures relating to the financial running of the hotel. After this internship period, Dean was transferred to Cincinnati, Ohio, where he became an assistant manager.

He was promoted to manager within a year, but in the meantime, Dean had to oversee front-desk, maintenance, and housekeeping staffs. He hired and trained them and handled personnel problems. Meanwhile, he was learning more about the financial aspects of running the hotel from his manager. Dean worked all shifts at this time: nine to five, three to eleven, or eleven to seven, with emphasis on the heaviest check-in and check-out times.

Dean worked as assistant manager for about a year and was then promoted to general manager in Dayton, Ohio. After a year, he was hired by Marriott as a sales manager. As such, he had to try to find clients who were going to stay at the hotel for more than one night, preferably least a week or even a month. This job involved making cold calls, researching corporations, and networking with companies to see if he could get their business. In the process, Dean did a lot of wining and dining of prospective clients. He enjoyed the work and continued it for about a year.

But Dean decided that he wanted to go back to hotel management and was promoted to a general manager position in Ann Arbor, Michigan. He remained in that position for about two years and was then hired by the Hyatt Regency in Chicago as an assistant manager.

This two-thousand-room hotel was the largest he had managed so far. There were actually three assistant managers who rotated schedules on a monthly basis. At the time, Dean thought that the 11 P.M. to 7 A.M. shift was difficult but interesting. Much of his work involved monitoring other employees to make sure they weren't sleeping in one of the many hiding places that such a large hotel would have. As you might guess, Dean has countless stories to tell about hotels at night and what goes on in the dark!

But this shift played havoc with Dean's sleeping habits. Not a born night owl, he was always tired when he got home and just wanted to sleep. Dean says, however, that sleeping during the day is not the same as sleeping at night. He never got restful sleep because it was never dark enough to block out the sun.

He also was distracted by the noises of the street traffic. And when he got up at about 5 P.M., he wanted to run errands, but he couldn't go to the bank or to certain stores because they were closed. His eating habits suffered on this shift, and he had virtually no social life. Dean was glad that this shift only lasted a year.

At this time, Dean again took a look at his future prospects. In retrospect, he had done very well and moved up the ranks quickly. But he was also considering the fact that he never got vacations, did not have a social life, and was always on call. At that point, he decided that he was probably not a night owl, and the hotel business was not what he wanted to do forever. He took the nine-to-five job at the bank. He was able to successfully transfer many of the skills he had acquired in the hotel business to a new line of work—one where he could finally get a good night's sleep.

Dean does think, however, that the hotel industry has many advantages for the right person. You can, with hard work, advance rather quickly and receive very good on-the-job training. You may have to relocate in order to advance, and you will definitely have to work different shifts.

Chefs and Cooks

Maybe you'd rather work in the kitchen as a cook or a chef. To a certain extent, both titles imply that the employees do the same thing: follow recipes, know about kitchen equipment, and arrange the food in an appetizing way.

The chef, however, is the most highly trained kitchen worker, often known for specially created dishes prepared and presented in an innovative way. Chefs plan restaurant and banquet menus and supervise other kitchen staff. Some hotels have coffee shops and fast-food restaurants that employ cooks who prepare much more limited fare. Kitchen workers in hotels are subject to late shifts, holiday work, and weekend hours.

Education and Training

You can start out as a short-order cook without a high school education and receive on-the-job training. However, in order to become a chef, you will need years of training and experience. You will have to undergo an apprenticeship program in a professional setting, such as a culinary institute, trade union, professional association, or college. The larger hotels may also offer training programs. Some training facilities include courses in supervision and management.

You will learn how to bake, broil, sauté, and grill food; plan menus; purchase and store foods; and keep sanitary conditions in the kitchen. When you complete your training, which may last three years, you will want to be certified by the American Culinary Foundation. This group sets the standards for the industry and assures the quality of your training.

You may be in the position to supervise other employees on the job. You could then be promoted to executive chef or kitchen, dining room, or restaurant manager. The executive chef supervises all sous-chefs, or assistant chefs, and cooks and is responsible for approving the menu. This position requires specific training, apprenticeship, and certification. The menu planner works closely with the executive chef and usually has to have a bachelor's or associate's degree.

Other Food Service Workers

Two possible scenarios exist for advancing in the restaurant business. In the first, you would start off as an assistant cook and work up to cook and then to chef. From there you could become assistant manager and then manager. Another route would be to start busing tables, become a waiter, then host, assistant manager, and manager. Other entry-level positions that can lead you up the ladder are cashier, baker, or kitchen assistant. With some experience and training, you might become a dining-room manager, pastry chef, or bartender. From there you might become an executive chef, menu planner, dietitian, or food service manager.

The host at a restaurant greets the customers at the door, maintains the reservations list, and escorts guests to their tables. A pleasant personality and good organizational skills are necessary for this position.

The kitchen assistant helps the cooks, chefs, and bakers in the mixing and preparation of ingredients. Buspersons clear the tables after the guests have left and set the tables for the next customers. During the meal, they refill water glasses and coffee cups. They also may help the waiters with other housekeeping duties.

Waiters and bartenders are needed nights, weekends, and holidays in restaurants. Waiters take orders, serve food and beverages, and prepare bills for customers. Depending on the restaurant, they may recommend wines and beverages, describe food preparation, and even prepare special dishes at the table. They check on customers to see whether they need anything and whether everything is satisfactory. Other duties, such as escorting customers to tables or cleaning tables and serving areas, may also be required.

Bartenders prepare drinks for the customers and often socialize with them. They must know how to mix drinks, order liquor and bar supplies, keep the bar attractive, wash glasses as needed, and prepare fruit and other drink condiments.

If you aspire to higher levels in the restaurant business, you may become the food service manager, who is responsible for setting quality, efficiency, and profitability standards for the restaurant. The food production manager supervises the kitchen staff and sets costs and standards for sanitation.

Education and Training

There are no real educational requirements for waiters and bartenders, although bartenders can take courses at bartending schools. On-the-job training usually suffices for either job. What is important for these jobs is a pleasant personality, a good memory, and patience. Since both jobs involve a lot of public contact, you have to like working with people and want to serve them efficiently.

Earnings

The food service industry truly does offer jobs for people of all education and training levels and rewards them according to merit, enthusiasm, creativity, and willingness to serve. However, if you work for tips, your base pay may be comparatively small.

Most waiters and bartenders work for a basic hourly wage plus tips. Therefore, the base pay may not be much more than about $6 an hour to start. You may, after some time, earn up to $8 an hour; those working in very elegant restaurants earn higher wages. If you do well, you might become a supervisor or work in banquet services or as dining-room manager.

Hourly median wages for bartenders, before tips, average about $7; for wait staff, $6. These figures may not be representative of the entire industry, but they may serve as a guideline. Workers who earn tips may be paid less than minimum wage as a base rate, providing the opportunity exists to reach or exceed minimum wage with tips.

The National Restaurant Association estimates that tips could raise your income by $20,000 to $30,000 a year. Uniforms and meals may also be supplied by the restaurant. Even though restaurants require shift work, this may be to your advantage. Students, homemakers, aspiring actors, and musicians have found working in restaurants a satisfying way to make a living, to meet interesting people, to receive valuable on-the-job training, and to work up the ladder if they choose.

Is the Hospitality Industry for You?

If you decide to work for a hotel, you should be computer literate, have good communication and math skills, and be patient. You should also develop a sense of humor, if you don't already have one. You will have to assume a great deal of responsibility and learn to do many things, but you can make a very good living in hotels and restaurants.

For those of you who may still be considering a career in the hospitality industry, you may want to take a look at what the industry is all about, what you might contribute to it, and what it may offer you. The word *hospitality* just about says it all: it means quality service to the guest, including comfort, courtesy, security, grace under pressure, personality, skill, reliability, and style. It also means that the customer is always right. And that means that you are there to see to it that the customer is satisfied with the room, the food, the cleanliness, the competence, and the friendliness.

There is a special mind-set in this industry, and it has to do with putting yourself in someone else's shoes. If you work in a hotel, for example, you have to imagine how tired and hassled travelers might be and how you can help to relieve the stress of being in a strange city in an unfamiliar setting. They might be there on business or for pleasure, but it is still sometimes stressful to get settled comfortably in new surroundings. Whether a guest is alone, part of a business team, or with family, he or she needs to be guided by the skillful hands of professional hotel personnel.

Travelers also expect a room with clean linens, air conditioning, color television, extra blankets, and—in more luxurious accommodations—a chocolate on the pillow. Experts in housekeeping see to it that weary travelers have all the supplies they need to have a comfortable stay at the hotel.

Many people who travel do so because they want to try new food experiences in new settings prepared in innovative ways. They may be tired of tuna sandwiches, burgers, and fries. They are looking for something special, and they will find it either in the restaurant of the hotel or somewhere in the destination city. Therefore, the chefs, waiters, and hosts are there to make sure that breakfast, lunch, and dinner are served on time, are presented with style, and, above all, taste good.

Qualifications

If you decide to make a career in the hospitality industry, you need certain personal qualities, as well as skills and training. You definitely want to have a feel for people's needs, especially when they might be under the stress of being in unfamiliar territory.

You must be able to adapt to people who have special needs, such as those who are in wheelchairs or who have special dietary needs. In addition, you need to understand people who are in a party mood and are looking for fun when you are dead on your feet and just want to go home to sleep.

Now is the time to measure your "hospitality index." Do you think you can put on a smiling face, meet the various needs of your customers, and make sure they are satisfied? Are you developing these skills now in your personal life? Are you working weekends or summers as a waiter or bellhop to find out what hospitality is all about?

Are you an outgoing person who looks after people at parties to see whether they are enjoying themselves? Do you see to it that they have enough to eat and drink? Do you make sure that they are comfortable and enjoying themselves?

If you have these qualities, you are a prime candidate for the hospitality industry. There may be a career for you there, especially if you are a night owl. Answer the following questions to see whether you are suited to hotel work:

1. Do you actively participate in the preparation of parties or special events in your home?
2. Do you like to cook or experiment with recipes?
3. Are you aware of what is going on in your community as far as concerts, special events, guest appearances, sporting events, or personal appearances are concerned?
4. Do you have a knack for making people comfortable, even in an unfamiliar environment?
5. Are you reliable, dependable, and eager to please?

If you can answer most of these questions positively, you are probably suited to a career in the hospitality industry.

For Further Information

To obtain more information, contact the following organizations.

American Culinary Federation
P.O. Box 3466
St. Augustine, FL 32085
www.acfchefs.org

The American Hotel & Lodging Association
1201 New York Avenue NW
Washington, DC 20005
www.ahla.com

American Hotel Foundation
610 South Belardo Road, Suite 650
Palm Springs, CA 92264

American Institute of Wine and Food
1550 Bryant Street
San Francisco, CA 94103
www.aiwf.org

Careers, Inc.
P.O. Box 135
Largo, FL 34294

Council on Hotel, Restaurant, and Institutional Education
1200 Seventeenth Street NW, Seventh Floor
Washington, DC 20036
www.chrie.org

Educational Institute of the American Hotel & Lodging
    Association
800 North Magnolia Avenue, Suite 1800
Orlando, FL 32803
www.ei-ahla.org

International Executive Housekeepers Association
1001 Eastwind Drive, Suite 301
Westerville, OH 43081
www.ieha.org

The National Restaurant Association
1200 Seventeenth Street NW
Washington, DC 20036
www.restaurant.org

CHAPTER FOUR

Helping Us with Our Health

All of us know how important good health is and how we rely on health care providers to be there whenever we need them. This is one career group that has always had to be on call day and night—to perform emergency surgery, to deliver babies, to heal wounds, to monitor patients' progress, to administer medicine, and to advise and comfort the loved ones of the patient.

Human health needs—from the cradle to the grave—occur and are taken care of at all times of day or night by a wide range of professionals who have specific responsibilities. However, the first specialist we think of when we are sick or injured is the doctor.

Doctors, in turn, rely on a number of other medical personnel, including physician assistants, nurses, technicians, laboratory personnel, technologists, and paramedics. These are highly skilled professionals who must attain a certain level of education, training, and experience to qualify for health care work.

Physicians

Let's start with physicians, who diagnose and treat illness and disease after conducting physical exams. They also work to prevent illness by advising patients about nutrition, lifestyle, and hygiene.

The physicians we will discuss are M.D.s, or doctors of medicine. Other physicians practice as D.O.s, or doctors of osteopathy. D.O.s diagnose and recommend therapy based on the premise that bone structure must be aligned for proper health.

Primary care physicians usually treat patients they see regularly, and frequently patients' families as well, for all their illnesses. Others, called pediatricians, specialize in children's health. Still other physicians specialize in a specific part or region of the body or in a type of disease. For example, physicians can specialize in heart disease, internal medicine, skin disease, oncology, neurology, obstetrics, urology, or otolaryngology. Or they may perform neurological, gynecological, plastic, thoracic, or general surgery.

Physicians work in clinics, hospitals, offices, health maintenance organizations (HMOs), and for the military—sometimes even in combat zones. All in all, about six hundred thousand physicians practice in the United States. They find jobs in large cities, suburbs, small towns, and rural communities.

If you work anywhere in the United States as an M.D., you will have to be licensed. This means that you must be a graduate of an accredited medical school, pass a licensing exam, and serve a residency for one to six years. You most likely will need a bachelor's degree from a four-year college or university to get into medical school.

While in college or at the university, be sure to study science courses, including biology, chemistry, biochemistry, anatomy, and physics. Also include in your course work communications skills, math, and social sciences. Knowledge of computers is also necessary for health care work.

In order to get into medical school, you will have to pass the Medical College Admission Test (MCAT). If you are admitted to medical school (the competition is keen), your course work will include physiology, microbiology, anatomy, and pathology. You will learn to observe patients in hospitals and will work with children, expectant mothers, people with serious injuries, or those with emotional problems. You will also begin to learn how to diagnose and treat illnesses.

After you have successfully completed medical school, you must pass an exam given by the National Board of Medical Examiners to become a resident. After your residency, you will have to be board certified by passing a test administered by the American Board of Medical Specialists.

There are twenty-four areas in which doctors can be board certified:

1. Allergy and immunology
2. Anesthesiology
3. Colon and rectal surgery
4. Dermatology
5. Emergency medicine
6. Family practice
7. Internal medicine
8. Neurological surgery
9. Neurology
10. Nuclear medicine
11. Obstetrics and gynecology
12. Ophthalmology
13. Orthopedic surgery
14. Otolaryngology
15. Pathology
16. Pediatrics
17. Physical medicine and rehabilitation
18. Plastic surgery
19. Preventative medicine
20. Psychiatry
21. Radiology
22. Surgery
23. Thoracic surgery
24. Urology

If you decide to teach in any one of these specialties or want to conduct research in them, you will probably need further study and academic degrees. From the time you are a resident and often long after, you may need to work split shifts, graveyard shifts, or even twenty-four-hour shifts.

What It Takes

What are some qualities that you need to become a physician? You will definitely want to be able to help people, willing to work under stress, able to work well individually and as a member of a team, and able to make decisions quickly if there is an emergency situation. If you are still in high school, be sure to take a broad base of courses, including English, computers, biology, chemistry, physics, and math. Your extracurricular activities in both high school and college may prove to be important in getting into medical school, where well-rounded personalities are considered valuable. Volunteer work in a hospital during breaks will give you a feel for hospital work.

Since you will, as a physician, often have to make life-and-death decisions, you should start early in your life establishing priorities, gathering information, making decisions, and following through. You may also want to determine how well you respond in emergency situations:

- Can you keep a level head when things go wrong?
- How do you react to a sick or injured person or animal?
- Do you have patience and understanding when people are suffering or in pain?
- Do you faint at the sight of blood?

How you answer these questions may help you to determine whether you should become a doctor.

The workload can also be grueling. During medical school, you will be studying long hours. As a resident, you may be working twenty-four-hour shifts. And, depending on your specialty, you may be doing shift work or be on call for the rest of your working life. After all, who can tell when a baby will be born?

Earnings

Although your education is long and hard, the rewards, both professionally and financially, can be great. Physicians are among the best paid of all professionals, and job prospects look good for the immediate future. The American Medical Association (AMA) lists $160,000 as the median annual income for physicians, depending on their specialties and where they work. Average annual salaries for residents range from $34,100 to $42,100 from the first through the sixth year.

Many changes may take place in the health care system in the next few years that physicians and health care providers will have to take into account. For example, there may be a rise in the need for geriatric care because American citizens are aging. Primary care physicians will always be needed. As long as we all have so many parts that can and do go wrong, we will need doctors to repair them.

Emergency Medical Physicians

Night owls are definitely needed in this demanding area of medicine. Emergency medical physicians are always subject to shift work, which has been cited as the number one reason why physicians leave emergency medicine. Emergency physicians also cite emotional and physical stress, family considerations, and workload pressures as reasons for leaving the emergency room. Although emergency medicine is now an official specialty, it is a relatively new one. Approximately eight hundred physicians graduate annually from the 101 emergency medicine residency programs in this country.

Profile of an Emergency Physician

Rebecca Roberts grew up in a very small town in the state of Washington. In fact, the town was so small that the telephone book was only three pages long. Nobody in her family had chosen health care for a career. They never went to a doctor except in cases of emergency. Her mother went to a doctor only once that Rebecca can remember. That was for a bleeding ulcer and only when it was too painful to ignore. She also remembers that her father went to see a doctor only when he'd had a heart attack. Rebecca herself only went to the doctor when she had to be immunized for school. So where did her desire to become a doctor come from?

During her sophomore year at the University of Washington as a philosophy major, a professor reminded her that there were no jobs available for philosophy majors, except maybe in law. She knew she didn't want to spend her life arguing, but she hoped to do something that would help others. Rebecca was good at science and math, and she wanted a career that both used her strengths and was absorbing. She thought being a doctor would fulfill those needs. She changed her major to medicine. Because she switched midstream, it took her five years to finish her undergraduate work instead of four. She had to take certain science courses, for example, that were not required for philosophy.

Then she had to attend four years of medical school and one year of internship. Rebecca had pretty much decided on family practice, but she spent one year in urgent-care medicine and then took her residency at the University of Chicago. She got there as a result of the National Physicians' Matching Program, which is a rather complicated, but nearly flawless, computerized system that places residents in the hospitals of their choice.

In many programs today, the internship and residency are combined with three years of emergency room experience and an additional three years of study. After such a program, you would be board eligible in emergency medicine. To become board certified, you have to take both written and oral exams, sometimes six months to a year apart.

These exams are given at precisely the same time at different sites, such as Chicago, Dallas, Los Angeles, and New York. Security is very tight at these exams. For example, Rebecca had to bring her driver's license and picture identification, and her signature was compared. Applicants have three opportunities to pass this test, but it is very expensive, especially when transportation to and from the testing site is factored in.

Six months to a year later, the applicants have to take oral board exams, which consist of seven cases and fake scenarios. They have fifteen minutes for each case—not a long time to prove their skills, but necessary to pass the test.

Rebecca passed all these tests and is now a senior physician in emergency medicine. She also serves as associate residency director for training programs for residents in the emergency room. As such, she works ten shifts per month and is also on call.

Shift work can be dangerous when you are dealing with life-and-death situations. Therefore, scheduling has to be done carefully in medicine, and Rebecca prepares herself for her work for every shift by getting up very early, working hard, and going to bed early whenever she has to work long shifts. She also allows time for catching up on sleep.

Even though Rebecca has many responsibilities, she seems to have fulfilled her early goals for choosing medicine as her life's work. She's a true night owl. Sleep deprivation and lack of a normal social life don't deter her from what she feels is important. After all, that is what being a night owl is all about, isn't it?

Physician Assistants

Physician assistants, or PAs, work with the physician or surgeon at odd hours of the day and night. But maybe you've never heard of physician assistants. That may be because the PA position was created in the 1960s because of the lack of primary physicians. In 1998, there were more than sixty-six thousand working PAs in the United States.

The functions you perform as a PA vary from location to location, but you will always be working under the supervision of a physician. You may also serve as an assistant in surgery. PAs are qualified to perform the following functions:

- Take medical histories
- Perform physical exams

- Order laboratory tests
- Diagnose illness
- Treat injuries

Education and Training

In 1999, there were 116 accredited PA programs in the United States. In order to be accepted into a PA program, you generally have to have completed two years of college and have gained some work experience in health care.

Most programs take two years to complete. You'll be in the classroom the first year and in a clinic, hospital, or doctor's office the second year. In the first year, your course work will include biochemistry, anatomy, disease prevention, and physiology.

In the second year, your clinical rotation will include primary care medicine, surgery, obstetrics, geriatrics, and emergency medicine. Almost 50 percent of the applicants to PA programs do have bachelor's degrees. When you are in college, study English, biology, humanities, social sciences, chemistry, math, and psychology.

After you have completed your course work, you will have to take a certifying exam given by the National Commission of Certification of Physician Assistants (NCCPA). When you pass the test, you will have the title of Physician Assistant-Certified (PA-C). To keep your certification, you must complete one hundred hours of certified medical education courses every two years and take a recertification exam every six years.

Like physicians, PAs work in hospitals, clinics, private practices of physicians, HMOs, and the military—in cities, suburbs, and rural areas. Also like physicians, PAs can specialize in such areas as emergency medicine, family practice, geriatrics, internal medicine, obstetrics/gynecology, or pediatrics.

As mentioned previously, however, PAs always work under the supervision of at least one physician. They also work within the scope of their expertise and the laws of the individual state.

The District of Columbia and all the states except Mississippi have licensing regulations concerning the practice of physician assistants. These specialists will also be exposed to shift work if the supervising physician is involved with flexible working hours or is on call.

Earnings

Salaries for PAs range from $47,000 to $65,000 a year, depending on location, specialty, and years of experience. The job prospects also look good through the year 2008. According to all indications, this career is filled with opportunity.

. . . .

Nurses

More traditional, perhaps, is the career of the nurse. When we think of doctors, we almost automatically think of nurses. And when doctors do shift work, nurses are right beside them. Nurses make sure that patients are comfortable, give them their medications, help physicians during treatments, and record symptoms and progress of patients. Nurses are found in hospitals, nursing homes, doctors' offices, private businesses, armed forces, government agencies, cities, and rural areas—wherever doctors are practicing medicine. Nurses who work in hospitals, in private duty, for the armed forces, and in companies that run on a twenty-four-hour basis are required to do shift work. For example, they often have to work weekends, evenings, graveyard shifts, and holidays.

Registered Nurses

Registered nurses have to graduate from an accredited program and pass a national licensing examination. If you choose to train as a registered nurse, you will have three options for obtaining the qualifications you need to become certified—two degree programs and specialized hospital training:

1. Associate Degree in Nursing (A.D.N.)
2. Bachelor of Science Degree in Nursing (B.S.N.)
3. Diploma

The A.D.N. is a two- to three-year program, usually offered through community or junior colleges. The B.S.N. degree is offered at colleges and universities and takes four or five years to complete. The diploma is issued through two- to three-year programs given in hospitals. As with other professions, nurses with the bachelor's degree will advance more quickly into administrative or supervisory positions. You will also need the B.S.N. if you want to earn a higher degree, conduct research, or teach.

As with other health care professions, education includes both classroom work and clinical training. Courses include anatomy, physiology, microbiology, chemistry, psychology, and nursing. Then you receive supervised training in a hospital setting.

Most nurses do end up in hospitals, including the emergency room. But hospital nurses may also be found in the operating room, in the intensive care unit, or in oncology. They administer the health care procedures as outlined by the supervising physician or surgeon for individual patients.

Many patients in private care need round-the-clock attention. Therefore, nurses in this situation expect shift work or rotating hours. These nurses are hired by families or agencies to take care of patients in their own homes, in nursing homes, or in hospitals. Jobs in home health care and nursing home care may increase because of the aging of America and the increased need to care for the elderly.

Licensed Practical/Vocational Nurses

Licensed practical/vocational nurses (LP/VN) work in the same places that physicians, physician assistants, and registered nurses work. They work under the supervision of the physician or registered nurse, and although their responsibilities may vary, the LP/VN is primarily responsible for bathing and feeding patients, taking blood pressure, and observing symptoms. Sometimes they are required to keep records and recommend patient care.

It will take about a year to complete both classroom course work and clinical training. You will learn nursing skills, anatomy, physiology, pharmacology, and medical-surgical nursing. You can complete this work at hospital-based schools, community colleges, and vocational centers. After you have successfully completed this program, you must pass a licensing exam to practice as an LP/VN.

About seven hundred thousand LPNs were working in the United States in 2000, and because of the overall nursing shortage, career opportunities are good for the immediate future. You have to be patient, flexible, reliable, and tactful to be an LPN. The median annual salary was $29,440 in 2000.

Occupational Health Nurses

Since many companies run on a twenty-four-hour basis, occupational health nurses (OHNs) are needed at work sites to ensure the health and safety of the employees. The larger the facility and the more dangerous the work, the more the OHN is needed on every shift.

The occupational health nurse should ideally be considered an important member of the management team. The individual company will decide the scope of the health and safety needs, the health programs required, the budgetary needs of the programs, and the number of nurses needed. Some factors used in the decision-making process may include the size of the company, the primary health and safety hazards, and the health and safety needs of the staff.

If, for example, an industrial company has three hundred employees, it should staff one OHN; however, three nurses may be required in an industrial setting with up to a thousand employees. These nurses will then be able to provide counseling for substance abuse or programs for quitting smoking, losing weight, or staying fit. They can monitor high-risk employees, teach the staff about safety precautions, act as liaisons with insurance companies, and give physical exams to the employees.

Nurses often join professional organizations that set standards of excellence for both education and research. These organizations recommend professional standards for registered nurses in this country, monitor government regulations and pending legislation related to nurses, and keep members informed of job openings.

....

Surgical Technologists

Other night owls working in health care are the surgical technologists who belong to the team of surgeons, anesthesiologists, registered nurses, and any other medical staff members who are present during surgery. Since people may need surgery at any time, surgical technologists are involved in shift work and are often on call for emergencies.

Training and Certification

In order to become a surgical technologist, you must successfully complete an accredited program offered at community or junior colleges, vocational schools, universities, in the military, or at certain hospitals. The program lasts from nine to twenty-four months depending on whether you want a diploma, certificate, or associate's degree.

Your course work will include medical terminology, anatomy, physiology, microbiology, and pharmacology. You will also learn about surgical procedures and instruments, fundamentals of surgical care, and techniques that are necessary to prepare for surgery. In order to become certified, you have to complete your course work and pass a certification test. As a certified surgical technologist, you would be working in hospitals, ambulatory care centers, clinics, surgical centers, and physicians' offices. You can further advance in your career by specializing in a particular type of surgery.

Forecast and Earnings

Your future looks bright into the year 2010, in some cases because of the aging of America. More surgeries may be needed as the population ages. Salaries vary according to where you live and how much expertise you possess. In 2000, the median annual salary for surgical technologists was $29,020.

···

Clinical Laboratory Technologists

Clinical laboratory technologists also fall into the category of night owls, for although they usually work forty hours a week, these hours may be worked in the evening or at night. Laboratories are often open twenty-four hours a day, seven days a week, so technologists may have to work weekends and holidays.

These specialists perform laboratory tests, usually under the supervision of a physician, to help detect the cause of disease. Their tests can then lead to diagnosis and treatment. Technologists conduct routine tests on blood, urine, spinal fluids, and virtually any human substance. They may also test for cholesterol levels, AIDS, or blood glucose. Many of these tests are complicated and may be either chemical or bacteriological in nature. Clinical laboratory technologists analyze the results of these tests and report them to the doctors. Some technologists may even choose to specialize, for example, in microbiology or blood banks.

Training and Certification

You may qualify as a medical technologist with a bachelor's degree in medical technology. If you are still in high school, you should concentrate on biology, math, chemistry, and physics. In college, your course work will include chemistry, biology, microbiology, and math. The Commission on Accreditation of Allied Health Education Programs, the Accreditation Bureau of Health Education Schools, and the National Accrediting Agency for Clinical Laboratory Sciences are recognized as official accreditation organizations for medical technologists.

As a medical technologist, you will work in the same places as the other health care professionals: in hospitals, HMOs, blood banks, doctors' offices, or independent laboratories. You may also work for private agencies or for the government.

Since there may be pressure on the job, you have to be calm, patient, and reliable. You must also be accurate, clear thinking, and detail minded. Sometimes the work can be routine, but you will also be learning new techniques all the time and should realize that your work is extremely important for the diagnosis and treatment of disease.

Forecast and Earnings

New home laboratory testing procedures and the use of equipment that eliminates the need for humans may influence the job growth rate, but since the general population is aging, there will be a built-in base of need in the future. Salaries depend on location, experience, and expertise, but recent figures show that the average median annual salary was $40,510 in 2000.

Emergency Medical Technicians

If you want to be in the health field but from a different angle, you might want to become an emergency medical technician (EMT). These are the health care professionals who have been called as a result of an accident, heart attack, poisoning, or knife or gunshot wound. They rush to the site in an ambulance (or sometimes even in a helicopter) and administer emergency care before transporting the patient to the hospital.

There are three categories of EMTs with varying areas of responsibilities:

1. **EMT-Basic.** These specialists bind wounds, resuscitate, stop bleeding, give oxygen, and assist in cardiac emergencies.
2. **EMT-Intermediate.** In addition to the basic skills, these EMTs can help with respiratory emergencies and administer shock treatments to patients whose hearts have stopped.
3. **EMT-Paramedic.** These professionals can also give drugs to patients and operate more complicated equipment.

EMTs are in constant radio contact with medical personnel at the hospital who advise them on more complicated procedures. Once they get the patient to the hospital, EMTs have to report exactly what they did and why. This job is often stressful because life-and-death decisions have to be made in a hurry and under pressure. People can be seriously injured, poisoned, burned, shot, or in the critical stages of a disease. In addition, EMTs are exposed to life-threatening diseases and must do strenuous lifting, moving, kneeling, and bending. They work irregular hours and are often on call for emergencies.

EMTs work for hospitals, at police and fire departments, or for private companies. In large cities, they are paid for their work; in small towns, they are often volunteers.

In order to become an EMT-Basic, you need training in cardiac and respiratory procedures and in assessing patients' needs. You will probably get on-the-job training in a clinical setting or ambulance. There you run the gamut from delivering babies to stopping bleeding to using emergency equipment. To become an EMT-Intermediate, you generally concentrate on cardiac and respiratory emergencies. To be an EMT-Paramedic, you must complete up to two years of advanced course work, pass the National Registry of Emergency Medical Technicians exam, and be certified by your state. You must also continue your education with seminars and workshops throughout your career.

Forecast and Earnings

Job opportunities look good to the year 2010, especially in hospitals and ambulance services, again in large part because the aging population may need more emergency services. Although earnings may vary depending on experience and location, the median annual salary in 2000 was $22,460.

Profile of an EMT-Paramedic

Rich Wood could be featured here or in the chapter about transportation night owls. He has worked as a truck driver but is now a paramedic in the Chicago area. He got started in 1972, when he was discharged from the army after serving in Vietnam. Although he had no medical experience at that time, he was concerned about his future. His father was a volunteer firefighter for about a year, and his grandfather was a professional firefighter for twenty-seven years and died on the job of a heart attack. But neither of them was in the ambulance service. So Rich did not think that this type of career was in his blood.

A friend of his was working for an ambulance company and encouraged Rich to take the training. At that time, a person had to attend eight hours of training in first aid with the Red Cross to work in the suburbs. But Rich decided to go for the forty-hour intensive training required for work in the city. His company paid for his training as part of his job working on an ambulance.

There were two people in the ambulance, and they would contact the police in an extreme emergency. The police would then contact the hospital and dispatch the ambulance to that hospital. The police might often block intersections or stop traffic so that the ambulance could get to the hospital as soon as possible. The ambulance personnel basically administered minimal first aid techniques, but the primary responsibility was to get the patient to the hospital for emergency care as quickly as possible.

At that time, they worked for minimum wage, which was $1.50 an hour plus overtime past forty hours a week. In order to make ends meet, most people were working a hundred hours a week. By that time, Rich was starting a family and sometimes working eighteen- and twenty-four-hour shifts—for example, on twenty-four hours, off eight, on twenty-four. That schedule didn't leave much time for family life. Although he was working nonstandard hours, Rich doesn't recall ever having a problem adjusting his inner clock. Since helping people who are in trouble is his driving force, he was ready to help whenever and wherever he was needed.

In 1974, Rich decided that he needed to switch jobs in order to earn more money. The job had many rewards, but they weren't monetary. He had started taking business management courses, and at a job fair he landed a job as a dispatcher for a trucking company. He advanced to lead dispatcher and then took a job in Boston with a different company for much more money. There he was operations manager for a small, long-distance trucking company that also leased to other contractors.

His second son came along, but his first son died in 1979. At this time, Rich had to rethink his life and career. He questioned whether he had spent enough time with his kids, especially since he had another child on the way—this time, a daughter. He remained with that job for a while but did eventually move to New Jersey and Philadelphia as a dispatcher. He was on call twenty-four hours, working 7 A.M. to 11 P.M.

When he spent time with his children, it was always for something special—going to Hawaii or New York City. But Rich let long stretches of time go by without much time off. His friends were the people he worked with. On the rare occasions when he went out, it was with his coworkers—so that they could talk shop!

He then moved to Delaware, where he was general manager for a trucking firm. He hired drivers, mechanics, and office managers and saw to it that the mechanics were trained in company procedures. He and a friend bought a trucking company that was in deep debt and had outdated equipment. The big investment of time required by the business caused his personal life to suffer. His many absences brought about a divorce. In 1988, for example, he figures that he was away from home 343 days, home 22 days.

Rich sold his company and moved back to Chicago. Since his children were grown, he didn't need as much income as he did when his family was together. That's when he decided he didn't want to be a manager anymore. He went back to school and got his EMT-Basic training. He studied for six months to get his certificate, which was a combination of classroom and ambulance work. Rich also continued to pursue business courses in hopes of getting his bachelor's degree in business.

He got his EMT certificate, worked for a company for a year, and was also driving a truck. As a truck driver, he would often work fifteen hours with an eight-hour break. The U.S. Department of Transportation dictates these rules. Sleep would be enjoyed either in the truck, if it had a sleeper, or in a motel. He could also take showers and rent rooms at truck stops.

Even with his grueling schedules, Rich has never had an accident. He always just goes to a truck stop or rest area to sleep if he needs it and recommends that for other drivers.

Rich admits that his nutritional habits are not very good as a result of his career choices. As a trucker, he rarely had time to sit down to eat; he got used to eating snacks and greasy fast food on the run and drinking lots of caffeine. Although the money was good as a truck driver, loneliness and isolation can occur. It was good to talk to others on CB radios and at truck stops to keep you alert and awake.

Rich eventually devoted less time to driving the truck and more time to school and working in the ambulance. He decided to go beyond the EMT-Basic training even though he had no idea how difficult that would be.

In order to qualify, he first had to take tests in first aid, airway management, bleeding, all basic skills. If you don't pass it, you just don't get in. Most hospitals and some local colleges offer these courses. Rich's training lasted for nine months, attending classes from 6 P.M. to 10 P.M., Monday and Wednesday. He had a lot of homework and a test every class period. At the end of every month, he took a modular test, and he had to pass each one. If he had failed two, he would have been dropped from the course. Then he was given applied and clinical time and time in the emergency room as well as classroom work. The teacher, the emergency room staff, and the primary care physician make sure that trainees know what they are doing; when they have ride time in the ambulance, the preceptor further assists and evaluates their skills. Eventually Rich stopped driving the truck and earned his income entirely from ambulance work.

He says that ambulances are so much more sophisticated than they were when he started. Back in 1972, if he had a patient with a heart problem, he would simply administer oxygen and get the patient to the hospital as quickly as possible. Now paramedics administer oxygen, monitor heart rhythms, test blood sugar, decide on drug treatment, start IVs, and defibrillate as needed. Rich works under a doctor's license with standing medical orders (SMOs) within a specific hospital system. The doctor issues these SMOs, and Rich reports to the hospital staff exactly what he has done and requests further advice or recommendations, thereby bringing the emergency room to the patient instead of vice versa.

Rich depends on his children, grandchildren, and friend Sherry to help him through stressful periods. He needs good listeners to vent about the situations that he has encountered during his shift. He also had an excellent instructor who helped him get through.

Now Rich is working to become a paramedic. He works for both a fire department and a private ambulance company. The fire department gives him a schedule on a weekly basis, sometimes requiring him to work forty-eight hours a week. It's not unusual for Rich to also work another forty-four hours for the ambulance company—and that's a slow week.

Rich hasn't noticed a great change in job security as a result of the recession, but he does say that he and other medical professionals have been receiving more courses dealing with disaster and interagency cooperation since September 11.

Rich is very happy in his work, in spite of the hours and the stress. The rewards are great, especially when he knows how much he has helped so many people in his work.

....

Pharmacists

At many all-night drug stores there are also many night-owl pharmacists. They work through the night for those minor and major medical emergencies that can happen to any of us. We all run out of medicine or need it in a hurry for a sick child or elderly person. To many people, pharmacists may look as if they simply empty pills into small containers after successfully interpreting the doctors' handwritten prescriptions. In reality, however, they are highly trained and licensed professionals who have studied for many years so that they can measure and mix the right drugs and medicines according to the doctor's instructions, as well as provide advice to clients about medications.

Training and Education

In most cases you have to be licensed to practice pharmacy after graduating from a college of pharmacy, serving an internship with a licensed pharmacist, and passing the state exam. There are eighty-two colleges of pharmacy accredited by the American Council on Pharmaceutical Education. Before being admitted, you might have to take the Pharmacy College Admissions Test.

While in college, you take a wide variety of science courses, especially chemistry, biology, and physics. In pharmacy classes, you learn how to mix compounds and dispense prescriptions, as well as how to manage your responsibilities. You also learn about ethics. After graduation, you must obtain a license in order to get a job as a pharmacist. Once you pass a state board exam, the amount of time you must intern under a licensed pharmacist varies from state to state.

You can also continue your education by earning an advanced degree. Master's and doctoral degree candidates study pharmaceutical chemistry, pharmacology, or pharmacy administration.

What to Expect

What do pharmacists do when they are on the job? Since many of the pharmaceutical companies manufacture premeasured pills, present-day pharmacists spend more time counseling their customers about the use of drugs, determining which medications can safely be taken with others, and learning about the customer's health history. Pharmacists also keep records of medications prescribed to their customers and keep track of all medicines those customers are taking.

Forecast and Earnings

Pharmacists who work in retail pharmacies should have no trouble finding jobs through 2010 because of the growing population, the aging of the population, and the fact that older citizens tend to require more prescription drugs. The median annual salary for pharmacists is $70,950.

Pharmacy Aides

Where there are pharmacists, there are pharmacy aides. They keep records, prepare insurance claim forms, and inventory medications. They also often act as cashiers. Because they work closely with pharmacists, especially in retail stores and hospitals, they often work evenings, weekends, and holidays.

You can receive on-the-job training for this career, but you should have at least a high school diploma. Some experience in customer service and communication skills helps. Pharmacy aides should be somewhat computer literate, too, in addition to having math skills.

Forecast and Earnings

Your job opportunities are good through 2010 because of attrition and the aging of the population. The median hourly wage was $8.52 in 2000, with higher salaries in hospitals.

For Further Information

A variety of publications are available from these organizations, and additional information is provided online.

American Academy of Physician Assistants
950 North Washington Street
Alexandria, VA 22314
www.aapa.org

American Association of Colleges of Nursing
One Dupont Circle NW, Suite 530
Washington, DC 20036
www.aacn.nche.edu

American Association of Colleges of Pharmacy
1426 Prince Street
Alexandria, VA 22314
www.aacp.org

American Medical Association
515 North State Street
Chicago, IL 60610
www.ama-assn.org

American Medical Technologists
710 Higgins Road
Park Ridge, IL 60068
www.amt1.com

American Nurses Association
600 Maryland Avenue SW
Washington, DC 20024
www.nursingworld.org

American Society for Clinical Laboratory Science
7910 Woodmont Avenue, Suite 530
Bethesda, MD 20814
www.ascls.org

American Society for Clinical Pathology
Board of Registry
2100 West Harrison
Chicago, IL 60612
www.ascp.org

Association of American Medical Colleges
2450 N Street NW
Washington, DC 20037
www.aamc.org

Association of Physician Assistant Programs
950 North Washington Street
Alexandria, VA 22314
www.apap.org

Association of Surgical Technologists
7108-C South Alton Way
Englewood, CA 80112
www.ast.org

Liaison Council on Certification for the Surgical Technologist
7790 Arapahoe Road, Suite 240
Englewood, CA 80112
www.lcc-st.org

National Accrediting Agency for Clinical Laboratory Sciences
8410 West Bryn Mawr Avenue, Suite 670
Chicago, IL 60631
www.naacls.org

National Association for Practical Nurse Education and Service
1400 Spring Street, Suite 330
Silver Spring, MD 20910
www.napes.org

National Association of Boards of Pharmacy
700 Busse Highway
Park Ridge, IL 60068
www.nabp.org

National Association of Chain Drug Stores
413 North Lee Street
P.O. Box 1417-D49
Alexandria, VA 22313
www.nacds.org

National Association of Emergency Medical Technicians
408 Monroe Street
Clinton, MS 39056
www.naem.org

National Commission on Certification of Physician Assistants
157 Technology Parkway, Suite 800
Norcross, GA 30092
www.nccpa.net

National Credentialing Agency for Laboratory Personnel
P.O. Box 25945
Lenexa, KS 66285
www.nca-info.org

National Federation of Licensed Practical Nurses, Inc.
893 U.S. Highway 70 West, Suite 202
Garner, NC 27529
www.nflpn.org

National League for Nursing
61 Broadway
New York, NY 10006
www.nln.org

National Registry of Emergency Medical Technicians
P.O. Box 29233
Columbus, OH 43229
www.nremt.org

CHAPTER FIVE

News, Views, and More

The Media Night Owls

When we say the word *media*, many ideas may come to our minds. We might think of the media as any source of communication, information, or entertainment. We may first think of television because it is right in our homes all the time, and we probably watch it more than we would like to admit.

Television provides news and weather reports; dramas and comedies; sporting events; home shopping programs; new and old movies; travel, science, and talk shows; live court action; educational programs; and cartoons. The number of channels grows every year. So television is a major component of the media because it provides us with communication, information, and entertainment. Newspapers, magazines, and radio also provide both news and entertainment.

All of us are greatly influenced by the various media that fill our days and nights with entertainment and information. We read, listen, and watch for hours every day because these media form the basis of the common knowledge that we receive and react to on a daily basis. In many ways, they shape our society and culture by providing us with the everyday information needed to form opinions, make decisions, and relate to our environment.

Who doesn't turn on a radio every day for the news, weather, traffic reports, or favorite music? Radios are now constant companions—thanks to inexpensive headsets—to joggers, cyclists, commuters, beachcombers. Who doesn't read a newspaper on the bus or train to work or spend hours on Sunday going through the comics, sports section, book reviews, fashion reports, and the hard news coverage and editorials?

And who doesn't spend a few hours after dinner watching sitcoms, news reports, movies, or made-for-TV dramas? Isn't that why the expression *couch potato* was coined?

Kids watch their favorite shows on Saturday morning, and game shows, talk shows, and soaps entertain those who are at home during the day. Cable TV has also opened up new possibilities for community and special-interest shows.

Many of us subscribe to specialty magazines that appeal to one or another topic of interest. Browse through the magazine section of a grocery, pharmacy, or bookstore and we can find magazines dealing with fashion, health, architecture, nutrition, hobbies, interior design, religion, music, art, news, business, travel, pets, bodybuilding, politics, food preparation, parenting, or mechanics.

Magazines may appeal to certain age and interest groups, such as children, women, or senior citizens. They may cater to ethnic groups or political affiliations. The range of topics in magazines is as broad and diversified as the range of human experience.

Who puts all of this together for us to be so informed and entertained? As you might expect, it takes many people of various talents, capabilities, and backgrounds to bring all this news, information, and entertainment into our lives. In addition to the various administrative, supervisory, and clerical personnel, the media need announcers, newscasters, reporters, producers, correspondents, writers, editors, designers, photographers, camera operators, technicians, artists, and printers. And many of these talented individuals are night owls. Let's take a closer look at some of these jobs to determine where you might fit in best.

Newspaper Reporters

If you have a knack for writing, you may want to become a newspaper reporter, editor, columnist, or correspondent. Your hub is the newsroom, which today is a highly automated place. Computers and satellites help bring the news to us every day.

The reporter's job is to go to where the news is being made—at the scene of a fire or a crime, at city hall, at a disaster area—and gather the facts by observing and interviewing key people. Who, when, what, where, and why—these are the five Ws every reporter brings back to the newsroom. If your assignment is to investigate people in government, you may have to thoroughly research public documents, attend public hearings, and interview the people involved.

Reporters may bring tape recorders and notebooks with them, and some may even use laptop computers on the scene and send the story by modem to the computer in the newsroom. Often photographers are assigned to accompany reporters to cover the stories. No matter which method is used, reporters are always working on deadline.

As a general assignment reporter, you are assigned to breaking news stories in a wide range of areas. You could write about a shooting one day (crime), investigate a chemical spill on a highway the next (environment and transportation), and cover a rally for the mayor another day (politics).

Other reporters assigned to specific "beats" specialize in particular areas of expertise—crime, politics, sports, business, real estate, religion, the arts, education, or science. Working as a reporter brings you into contact with a wide range of people and events. Some of the stories you cover will be sad or tragic, such as fires, floods, murders, or disasters. Others will be joyful and uplifting, such as personal triumphs over physical or emotional obstacles, communities working together to rebuild after a natural disaster, or a rescue team that has successfully removed a child from a dangerous situation.

Reporters who work for morning newspapers generally have to work the four-to-midnight shift or the graveyard shift. Radio and TV reporters work days or evenings. Most reporters are always on call, however, because of deadlines or because news breaks at any time. Reporters on smaller newspapers may have to perform a variety of tasks, including taking photos, writing headlines, or laying out pages. Regardless of the medium, the primary requirements for a reporter are the ability to gather facts, analyze them, and write so that the public can understand the events that take place every day and, as a result, be able to form opinions and make decisions about those events. Reporters play a vital role in our society, especially in guaranteeing one of our most valuable rights—the freedom of the press.

Working in journalism can be a lifelong career, or it can be a stepping-stone to managerial, political, teaching, or public relations positions. The experience gained is useful in many careers.

Training and Education

What should you do to become a reporter, columnist, or correspondent? It's a good thing to write as much as you can. Study liberal arts in college and work as a summer intern if possible. Work on your school newspaper, and talk to reporters to see what the job is really like.

A bachelor's degree in journalism is usually preferred, but a degree in a specific area, such as political science, could put you in a good position for becoming a specialist. You might also take a course in television newscasting. Computer literacy is vital for these careers.

Let's take a closer look at each of the training recommendations to see if they fit you and your career aptitude.

Practice Writing. What should you write? Anything and everything. Write research papers; write for religious or community groups; write for your school newspapers; write book or movie reviews; write about sporting events; write in your journal or diary.

Study Liberal Arts. You should also try to get the broadest kind of education, with emphasis on English and foreign languages, sociology, economics, political science, history, computers, and journalism. The same type of course work will be helpful in high school. Some journalism courses may include ethics, basic reporting, copyediting, and the history of journalism.

Gain Experience. Both in high school and in college, you will have opportunities to work on your school newspaper. You may not only write for these publications but also learn how to edit or even manage. During the summer vacations, be sure to apply for the internship program on your local newspaper.

Learn from Reporters. While working as an intern, get to know as many reporters, editors, and photographers as possible. Learn as much about their jobs as you can; that is, gather the facts, analyze them, then decide if the newsroom is the place for you.

Work Pressures

Remember that a reporter is under constant pressure to meet deadlines, and the pressure of shift work adds to the stress of a reporter's job. Although there may be a pay differential for night work, the adjustments of the social and biological rhythms associated with shift work may not always compensate for the additional pay. But, as with any other career that you love, most reporters would probably not give up the job for a little more sleep.

Forecast and Earnings

Because of many recent mergers, growth in these careers may see a slowdown through 2010. Competition for these jobs is always high, but in a recession, only the best will be hired. Vacancies will, however, occur as the population ages and veteran newscasters and reporters retire.

Your salary depends on whether you work for a large operation or a small station, in a large city or small town. Median annual earnings for news analysts, reporters, and correspondents were $33,550 in 2000.

··············

Editors

But perhaps you'd like to think about becoming an editor. First we'll take a look at what an editor is, and then we'll look at the different kinds of editors. Editors for any of the media must have an excellent command of the English language, a keen mind for detail, and a sharp eye for error in fact or discrepancy in logic. Editors also may have to deal with budgetary needs and should have an ability to motivate others on the staff to do their best.

City editors assign stories to reporters and decide which stories should be emphasized. City editors function as key players in the newsroom, having to make decisions quickly, and they need a challenge in their work.

Copyeditors check written text, or "copy," for errors in grammar, writing style, and fairness in presentation. They may also be required to know something about photo editing and layout.

Feature editors assist in the development of stories that affect the readers' emotions in some way. These specialists are interested in human behavior and motivation, as well as lifestyles. Newspapers may also have specialty editors for food, sports, movies, the arts, and education. Editorial page editors record the newspaper's philosophy, opinion, and beliefs. Sometimes they endorse political candidates; sometimes they draw attention to injustice, corruption, or graft in government, the courts, corporations, or even the educational system.

Managing editors oversee the daily operation of newsrooms and generally work daytime hours unless a major story is breaking. These professionals know not only what good copy and writing style are all about, they also have to know about each of the functions of the newsroom, understand how to motivate people, and want to make a difference in the community.

Training and Education

Many editors started out as editorial assistants, research assistants, or trainees. Writers and editors need highly developed research skills, and it's a good idea to have a wide range of knowledge and interests. They may also be required to understand layout, graphics, and interviewing techniques. Computer skills are also a must now in the newsroom.

You should have a college degree to become a writer, editor, or reporter. Most employers prefer a degree in English, journalism, or communications. If you decide to specialize in business, religion, or politics, you should also take courses in English, journalism, and communications.

Photographers and Graphic Artists

If news breaks in the middle of the night, a newsroom needs more than reporters and editors to get the story out on time. News photographers and artists also work to bring the facts of the story to life. Most of us in the twenty-first century have become accustomed to some sort of graphic representation either to supplant the printed word or to complement it. Photographers have done a great deal in the past century to help us see and interpret the newspaper's words in a different light and perspective. In fact, we have become accustomed to the "picture that is worth a thousand words."

News photographers have to be where the news breaks whenever that happens. It could be in their own hometowns or halfway around the world. It could be a war or a major sporting event. It could be a terrorist bombing in New York, an economic summit in Italy, or peace negotiations in the Mideast. News can happen at any time and any place, and photographers are there to record it.

Photographers, who take still photographs, and camera operators, who operate video and movie cameras, not only have to develop a feel for the story, they also have to be technically proficient with cameras and their various paraphernalia. Photographers generally use 35 mm or digital cameras. Camera operators often use steadicams that are strapped to their shoulders to provide stability to the camera.

Graphic artists create images that represent elements of the news, such as an earthquake, fire, courtroom scene, or police emergency. They use desktop computers to design maps, charts, tables, and even cartoons. Computer graphics are now much needed in newsrooms for informational graphics. These graphics might depict how something was done as well as where it happened. They also may represent a certain perspective or collection of events to be analyzed. A good news artist has the ability to visually depict or back up a story with computer-generated graphics, coupled with the ability to work with reporters and editors to help tell the story or represent the facts.

Graphic artists also do page layout for newspapers to clearly and artistically present the whole story—text and graphics. In order to do that, the designer must understand typography and the skillful use of photos, maps, and diagrams. Page designers have to know about the news as well as about art.

Training and Education

You would do well to take some photography classes at either community, junior, or four-year colleges to become a photographer or camera operator. Working in a camera shop during summer vacations, taking photos at family gatherings, or working on your high school yearbook will give you some experience with photography, film, and photo techniques. You will then receive on-the-job training at newspapers or TV and radio stations.

As with most other professions, however, the more formal education you receive, the more opportunities you will have to get a better job with more possibilities for advancement. That education, along with practical experience, will put you in a good career position.

Be sure to hone your computer skills, including familiarity with graphics software. Learn about production, design, and technical rendering. Keep your eyes open for photo opportunities and take pictures of everything. Or, if you are an artist, draw them. Just as writers must write, photographers and graphic artists must expand their visual possibilities in order to succeed. You'll have to be able to tell a story with your pictures, capture the dramatic moment, and communicate feelings for the event. This will take practice, but you will have many career opportunities with the media if you develop these skills.

Forecast and Earnings

The outlook for photographers and graphic artists looks good through the year 2010, but because competition is keen, you must have excellent skills and be highly motivated.

Salaries for photographers and graphic artists vary from location to location and with the size of the newsroom. Larger cities and facilities generally pay more than suburban or rural locations, but the smaller markets give you valuable experience and a foot in the door of your profession.

Radio and Television Announcers

Probably the most visible or audible people to those of us watching or listening are the announcers. These people may be called anchors, disc jockeys, talk-show hosts, sportscasters, weather forecasters, or commentators. They are all vital links between us and the outside world. We often pick our favorites and listen to or watch them on a regular basis. Style, appearance, voice, attitude, and even sense of humor bring us back to them. They eventually become a major part of our daily lives, and if they leave the station or network and go somewhere else, we invariably find them. They can and do have very loyal fans.

Since many networks have twenty-four-hour news programs, news analysts and commentators are also subject to shift work. News analysts sometimes specialize in certain areas, such as sports, while others are generalists. If you interpret the news and offer your opinion on the news, you are called a commentator or columnist. News analysts are usually reporters who read the news stories and present any prerecorded interviews to the listening or viewing audience. Often they present their stories live at the scene and are asked by the anchor to analyze the event. This often happens with natural disasters, fires, or accidents.

Disc jockeys often become so popular that they could be called cult figures. They're the ones who play the music we like the best, read the commercials, sometimes give us the news and weather, often host guest interviews, and always inject their personalities, comments, and opinions into their time slots. That's when we really get to know them and begin to build our loyalty to them. They are usually glib and can fill in the time with amusing and informative banter about a wide range of current events and popular opinions.

The people who predict the weather are called meteorologists. Their information is usually received from national satellite transmissions or from local weather sources.

Sportscasters can report live from the locker room, stadium, golf course, or tennis court. They may cover the Olympics or the World Cup at sites throughout the world. Or they may be assigned to the local Little League game or the high school volleyball championship. They often conduct postgame interviews with key players or coaches and offer commentaries on strategy and game plan. Their work may be presented live or on tape.

Radio stations and television networks also offer viewpoints and opinions about events that take place locally, nationally, or internationally. Since news anchors are supposed to present the news—that is, without injecting their personal opinions on the news—these opinions are expressed by commentators. Analysts and reporters may serve as commentators, but they must tell the listeners or viewers when they are acting as commentators. Many news shows have a specific segment that is devoted to nothing but opinion, but that is clearly stated at the outset of that segment.

The Work Experience

Radio stations and television networks are generally on twenty-four hours a day, so media people should expect some shift work.

Many disc jockeys and talk-show hosts work through the night; some handle the very early morning shift. The same problems of sleep deprivation and loss of some social life can, therefore, bring stress into the workplace.

Again, if you are doing what you love, you will find other rewards. One may be fan loyalty. Another may be the recognition and esteem that you earn in the community. Still another may be your ability to influence and enhance people's lives through your insights, personality, or trustworthiness.

Training and Education

How do you get to be an announcer? There are a few paths open to you if you choose radio or television announcing. Let's start with courses you should seriously consider taking while you are in high school. You should definitely master English—grammar, pronunciation, and writing. Speech and drama classes, public speaking, and even foreign languages also will be valuable.

If you think you may want to be a sportscaster, start now to learn about different sports and sports figures. If you want to be a disc jockey, start learning about music, including instruments and famous musicians. Learn to differentiate the various kinds of music, such as country, rap, rock, folk, big band, jazz, and rhythm and blues. Or, if you prefer classical music, know the difference between an opera and an operetta, Domingo and Carreras, Mozart and Wagner, a symphony and a concerto.

If you want to be a news anchor, read newspapers and news magazines and become familiar with current events. If there are apprenticeship programs at your local radio stations or TV networks, apply to work with them during summer vacations.

Cable TV has expanded the opportunities for public access programs, which are often locally produced. These may offer opportunities for students during weekends or summers. They may even offer financial assistance for further study or on-the-job training. In other words, your time outside the classroom and in extracurricular activities can be used as learning time, too.

After high school, you may want to enroll in a four-year college or broadcasting school. A bachelor's degree in journalism, broadcast journalism, communications, or telecommunications would be advisable. Be sure to check the credentials of any technical school before you enroll, and consider also community colleges for the courses you may need.

What It Takes

As important as all your degrees, diplomas, and certificates, however, are some personal qualities, such as personality, voice, and, for TV, appearance. To demonstrate these qualities, you will probably be asked to submit an audition tape, either video or audio, to be considered as an announcer. But don't be surprised if you have to work your way up to being an announcer, beginning perhaps as a production assistant, reporter, research assistant, or interviewer.

Timing is everything in the broadcast studio, and you will have to be able to present your story in specific sound bites. You may also have to work under the pressure of deadlines. Your facility with English has to be excellent, and your knowledge of the local, national, and international scene has to be constantly updated, especially in your specific field—music, weather, sports, or news.

Career Paths

Because of the rapid revolution and advances in technology, new networks and cable systems may provide more work for radio and television announcers. As an entry-level broadcaster, you may want to start in radio and then branch out to other media, keeping in mind that, overall, communications is a highly competitive field. You may want to get some solid experience in the smaller markets, prove yourself as a capable announcer, and then try for the larger radio stations and television studios.

Earnings

Network announcers can command fairly high wages, so the competition is fierce for the top jobs. You may have to be patient and work for smaller stations at first where you can develop your skills, style, and basic abilities before you are on the air.

It is difficult to talk about salaries because they differ considerably, depending on whether you are working in radio, network, or cable TV. Salaries vary as much by where you work—whether in a small town or a large city—as by your training and experience. You may start out with not too much money in your paycheck, but the possibilities of becoming a player in the national networks is always there if you are willing to work hard for it.

Behind the Scenes: Technicians and Engineers

Behind the scenes at the station or studio are less visible people, but they are no less important than the anchor. These are the broadcast technicians, without whom we would never get the news, sports, weather, or music. These highly skilled professionals are responsible for installing and operating the equipment that makes the programs possible. This equipment includes cameras, microphones, lighting, sound effects, tape recorders, and film editors. This is all done in the control room of the station or studio.

From the control room, technicians move from camera to camera, from taped to live presentations, signaling directions to others with their hands or through headsets. Their job is to assure that the mechanics are in place so the programs can be transmitted.

There are various types of technicians (also called operators or engineers), each with specific functions. For example, there are audio and video control engineers as well as recording engineers. These technicians control the quality of sound and picture and make sure the correct sound effects are produced through the operation of specialized equipment. Other technicians keep the equipment in good condition through repair and servicing.

Chief engineers generally supervise the engineering and other technical personnel, but in cable television they have additional responsibilities. For cable, they are in charge of all technical work involved in cable system design, equipment, layout for communications service, standards for all equipment and materials, and construction of facilities. They also may make suggestions for new products, assist in marketing, advise on matters of franchise renewal, and help in budget preparation. You would need a degree in electrical engineering or comparable experience to qualify for this position.

The chief technician supervises all the technicians and is responsible for assuring the highest quality signal delivery of satellite and microwave relays to the head end. The head end holds the antennae that broadcast these signals. As supervisors, these technicians set quality standards for the staff's performance and handle all personnel problems, including salary reviews. Requirements for this position include a background in the industry and electronic training, plus experience in the field.

Training and Education

If you want to become a technician, it is a good idea to get formal training at a technical school, community college, or four-year college. Your degree should be in broadcast technology, although for some jobs, a degree in electronics or engineering would apply. In high school, take classes in math and electronics, develop hobbies that allow you to learn about electronics and electronic equipment, and develop good hand-eye coordination.

If you operate transmitters, you will have to get a permit from the Federal Communications Commission (FCC). You will also receive further on-the-job training from more experienced technicians once you are hired. And you will almost certainly start out at smaller stations where you will gain valuable experience and training so that you can advance to the larger studios.

Forecast and Earnings

Salaries vary according to location (with the larger markets paying the highest salaries), experience, position, and training.

Producers, Directors, and Managers

Producers may be called on to select the cast, schedule rehearsals, write scripts, and direct the camera staff regarding shots, angles, and cameras.

Assistant directors' responsibilities include putting the proper equipment in place before production, timing the show, and working with the director and crew during the show. These positions require bachelor's degrees in communications and some previous experience in production. The floor manager acts as liaison between the control room and the cast.

Cable TV is proving to be formidable competition to the major networks. It is a "boom" that is surely here to stay. Part of the reason is the diversity of programming available, including community shows, twenty-four-hour news programs, old and new films, home shopping programs, sporting events, and nature shows. Cable TV programs, such as major sporting events, can also be telecast simultaneously throughout the world. Don't forget to investigate cable stations as you begin your job search.

Training and Education

Nontechnical positions require a bachelor's degree in business administration, with emphasis in marketing, advertising, or finance, as appropriate to the position. A bachelor's degree in communications or telecommunications, specializing in journalism, radio and television, or communications media, would be appropriate for editorial and other nontechnical positions.

Profile of a Television News Writer/Producer

One of the first things you notice about Tim Jackson, a writer/producer for a Chicago TV station, is his great voice. Right away, you think that he must be an actor, announcer, or news anchor; his voice fills the room with a beautiful sound. But when he was younger, Tim says, he was just considered loud! Well, Tim took that voice (and various other skills) and made an exciting career for himself in radio and television.

As a teenager, Tim had his first night-owl job, but he hated the hours. He vowed never to work overnight again. Then, when he was just seventeen, he was doing voice-overs for commercials even though he'd had no formal speech courses. His uncle had encouraged him, though, which eventually led him to doing literally thousands of hours of voice-overs for the Northern Trust Bank's industrial training program, which consisted of cassettes and slide shows.

Tim attended college in New Jersey, where he studied liberal arts, public speaking, and theater. After taking a year off, he continued his education at Columbia College in Chicago, where he studied broadcasting and writing. While there, Tim worked as an intern for a local radio station. He was a general, all-round gofer, but he also learned to write and edit promotional copy and assist the producer.

But Tim's first real dream was to be a radio disc jockey. Tim loved music and thought it would be his niche. After many rejections, however, this rather sensitive person decided this was not for him. He took a job as an overnight assignment editor at the radio station, where he continued to learn new skills and gain valuable experience.

He later accepted the news bureau chief position for a new satellite news project—a joint venture of Westinghouse and ABC-TV. It was intended to be competition for the emerging CNN headline news shows. Tim had a five-state territory to build in a somewhat hostile environment.

Because the new venture wanted its affiliates to provide the product free of charge, Tim met with a great many problems. He was working impossibly long hours, seven days a week, and his work was mostly administrative. Administrative work was not what he really wanted to do because he had other talents that he wanted to utilize, not the least of which was that voice. And by this time, he knew he wanted to be a news writer and producer.

He had produced and written several late-night radio shows, cowritten live entertainment shows, and produced radio specials. So after nearly a year with the satellite news project, which folded after about fourteen months, Tim was looking for a job.

He had applied for a job at his current television station more than once, but this time he got lucky. They offered him a job as a news writer working from 4 A.M. to noon. So even though as a teenager Tim vowed never again to work the night shift, the career that he loves brings him back to nights all the time. From his many years in both radio and television, he has become accustomed to every imaginable shift, including 6 A.M. to 1 P.M. and 1 A.M. to 9 A.M., wherever there is a demand.

What does Tim now find so appealing about working at night? First, he is an independent, creative, and imaginative person—all qualities needed for the overnight shift. Since there may not be as many people on the overnight staff, he has to wear many hats. For instance, he has to know how to write interesting copy, how to match up the words with the graphics, and how to put together the best possible product under the pressure of tight deadlines.

Producers also must keep up with the latest and ever-changing technological advances in computers, cameras, and telephone systems. For example, WGN was one of the first TV news studios to use the computer. When Tim was hired, he was not computer literate and had to learn very quickly. He advises anyone who is coming into this business to learn as many computer systems as possible and to become familiar with both PC and Macintosh systems, notebook and desktop platforms, and be willing to learn new programs as they became available.

Advantages and Disadvantages. Tim believes that he has received more opportunities by being willing to work the grave-yard shift because there is less competition for these jobs and therefore more possibilities to be resourceful. But if you are looking at overnight work because of the pay differential, you are going into it for the wrong reason. It simply isn't that big.

One advantage, though, is that there is generally no top-level management working the overnight shift, so you can be independent, self-reliant, and creative in your work. Tim also likes not having to fight rush-hour traffic and being able to make appointments during the day with comparative ease.

You will not be surprised, however, if Tim lists sleep deprivation as one of the major disadvantages of overnight work. He also cites isolation, lack of patience, and burnout of the senses as some of the problems with night work. He advises night owls to take frequent naps and breaks and to watch out for weight gain.

Tim also suggests that anyone interested in radio or television news writing, reporting, or producing should get a good, solid education. Today's employers are looking for people with at least a bachelor's degree, and a master's degree is even better. What does he recommend studying as an undergraduate? He suggests communications, writing, history, political science, law, and literature. And because of the global implications in news reporting, Tim says, studying foreign languages, living in foreign countries, and knowing world geography are also becoming more and more necessary. He also emphasizes reading, preferably the classics, and writing, writing, writing if you want to be successful in this field.

Future Trends. What do you have to look forward to in the near future as far as working conditions are concerned? Tim believes that you will have to be computer literate and be willing to work flexible hours. He sees a trend toward hiring more part-time employees because more and more employers are unwilling to pay benefits. And although more opportunities will arise, there will probably be more work for less pay.

He also says that you should know that this business is market driven; that is, it supplies the product for the demand. For instance, if you want to be a network news anchor, you have to be aware that your "look" is sometimes as important as, or in some markets more important than, reportorial skills. And the "look" can change overnight.

The need for night owls may also dry up if the demand dries up. Overnight shifts are important as long as people want to hear the news, weather, or music on the morning drive. If the public no longer wants or needs that, you'll be working the day shift. But if you love this work, as Tim obviously does, the hours won't matter. As long as you have the energy to put out a new product every day that is as creative as you can make it, you'll do well in this field.

New Technology Careers in the Media

Newspapers and television and radio stations all need creative employees. Cable TV is opening more and more opportunities for careers, and interactive technology will offer new challenges in the future for the crossover of news and entertainment media. Some newspapers and magazines are already interactive, thanks to the networking system that links so-called global villages and creates a multimedia environment. This networking on the information superhighway is creating new job possibilities now and will continue to do so in the future.

Finding a Job

Some recommendations for finding jobs in the radio and television industry are the following:

- Look in your telephone book for networks in your area.
- Check the Internet for detailed information on professional organizations.
- Go to your local library and look for industry publications that may list job openings.
- Talk with people who already work in the industry, especially those who have the kind of jobs you're looking for.
- Talk with representatives at job fairs at school or at work.

- Find out from local stations if they have internships programs for students during summer vacations.

Somewhere, in all these areas, there are jobs for night owls. Be sure you find the job you want, and the hours will follow.

....

For Further Information

For more information, visit the websites for these organizations. You'll find details about membership, career opportunities, and a variety of publications.

Accrediting Council on Education in Journalism and Mass
  Communications
University of Kansas
School of Journalism
Stauffer-Flint Hall
Lawrence, KS 66045
www.ku.edu/nacejmc

Dow Jones Newspaper Fund, Inc.
P.O. Box 300
Princeton, NJ 08543
www.dj.com/newsfund

National Association of Broadcasters
Career Center
1771 N Street NW
Washington, DC 20036
www.nab.org

National Newspaper Association
1010 North Glebe Street, Suite 450
Arlington, VA 22201
www.nna.org

Newspaper Association of America
1921 Gallows Road, Suite 600
Vienna, VA 22182
www.naa.org

Newspaper Guild
Research and Information Department
501 Third Street NW, Suite 250
Washington, DC 20001
www.newsguild.org

Society of Broadcast Engineers
9427 North Meridian Street, Suite 305
Indianapolis, IN 46260
www.sbe.org

CHAPTER SIX

Let Them
Entertain You

Life would be dreary if all we had to do was work, even when we love our work. The daily routine of waking up to that dreaded alarm clock, drinking our coffee, taking a shower, figuring out what we'll wear, getting on the train or bus, sitting at our desk all day, going home, fixing dinner—or breakfast, if you're a night owl—getting ready for the next day, and going to bed can be tedious on a regular basis.

And even though night owls don't always have "normal" weekends off, they do look forward to their days off to relax, catch up on sleep, go to a show, attend a concert, or rent a movie. Whether the "weekend" comes on Saturday and Sunday or Monday and Wednesday, most working people do think about the weekend during the workweek as a time to refresh their bodies and rejuvenate their minds.

For some, it even becomes a matter of living for the weekend. And before it arrives, they have planned for it by discussing it with friends and family, buying tickets to the theater or concert, and making dinner reservations. Or they rush to the video rental store right after work to be sure to get their favorite movies. Or they hurry home to watch their favorite TV shows.

Some people even subscribe to a series of opera or ballet tickets just to be sure that leisure time entertains them in their preferred form. And the movie houses are packed as soon as a new movie comes out.

On those precious weekends, we can escape into another world of excitement, glamour, adventure, thrills, beauty, and special effects. All of these things come to us via the wonderful world of entertainment, including movies, plays, television shows, opera, concerts, ballet, night club performances, music festivals, and musical comedies. The variety of available choices only makes it more difficult to decide what to do in our free time. But somehow, even with all these choices, we are able to find something to amuse or entertain us.

That's when we are grateful to the actors, dancers, musicians, theater managers, projectionists, producers, directors, stagehands, ushers, concession attendants, and box office attendants. They allow us to forget for a short while all the problems, stresses, and worries of the workweek. They take us outside of our small worlds and help us to enjoy the pleasures of artistic talent and professional achievement. And they make it possible for us to return to the routine of the workweek more relaxed and invigorated.

Since most plays, operas, concerts, and dance performances are at night, we have many night owls to thank for making our lives more pleasant. Movie houses are open at night, as well as nightclubs and music halls. Actors, dancers, and musicians may rehearse during the day, but the show goes on at night, and often into the wee small hours of the morning when the rest of the world is just getting up.

Now if you have an inkling, a talent, or an itch to get into show business, there are a lot of possibilities open to you. For some jobs, you need artistic talent as well as training or education. For others, you might have to acquire supervisory, technical, or organizational skills. But if you want to be in show business, you will soon realize that there's no business like it in the world. So let's look at the opportunities available to you as a night owl.

. . . .

Actors

Probably everybody at one time or another has had the fantasy of being a star, either in the movies, on Broadway, or on a favorite television show. Maybe just for a day it would be fun to see ourselves on the big or small screen or imagine ourselves before a live audience applauding the performance and shouting for more.

Or perhaps we see ourselves in a huge house in Hollywood with a garage full of expensive cars and closets full of fabulous clothes. Everywhere we go, our fans would follow, begging for an autograph. Photographers would hound us for an exclusive picture for their magazines or newspapers. We would be on all the television talk shows, and everyone would love us.

Is this a realistic picture of the working actor, or do only a few talented people fit into that scene? And would you be one of them? Let's take a look at what is involved in becoming that star and living the lifestyle of an actor.

What It Takes

You have to have some talent that can be developed in order to succeed in the competitive world of show business. You need to be able to interpret your character, memorize your lines and stage directions, and take instructions from your director. You have to be able to bring your own life experiences or ability to understand human emotions and reactions to your role and know how to use your facial expressions, gestures, and movements to convey feelings to the audience.

For some roles, you may have to display your singing voice or your dancing feet. Still others may require great physical agility and fitness. Some plays will take place in a modern setting; others may be set in some other century, country, or entire civilization. Some scenes may take place in outer space or in a totally imaginary location.

You may have to research a major historical event or person in order to understand your role. You may have to juggle, fence, swing from the rafters, or play the saxophone.

Your role may require wearing costumes that you could never imagine yourself in. Or you may have to work with strange or awkward props or talk to someone who isn't there. You may be called on to portray a physically or mentally impaired person.

You may have to memorize hundreds of lines or just serve as a walk-on with no lines. You may play the leading role or a supporting character. More likely, you may start out as an extra, as part of the crowd in movies or plays. Extras are hired through a casting agency, which supplies movie studios with the number and types of people they need for that particular movie.

What to Expect

Stardom doesn't come easily, and those fancy cars don't appear overnight in your garage. Many actors, even very talented ones, have to support themselves with some other job or jobs while they establish their reputations. Still others may wait for years before they get steady work. Actors have traditionally worked as part of the wait staff in restaurants. However, in difficult times, when both the hospitality and entertainment industries are suffering, actors are hit doubly hard.

And since you may have to wait long periods of time between acting jobs, you need to develop patience. Your jobs will depend on auditions, so you must be able to present your talent under pressure and in a comparatively short period of time. The threat of rejection is always hanging over the head of the actor.

Therefore, you will also have to both develop thick skin and maintain your faith in your talent and training. Overnight sensations are rare in this field. Usually actors have to labor in bit parts and infrequent jobs before they begin to get reliable employment.

In the chapter on communications, we discussed the fact that news anchors have to have a "look," and that "look" may be fleeting. This may happen with acting, too. Appearance is very important on the stage and in movies, especially if you want to be a leading man or woman. However, the range of character or supporting roles is much broader and allows for many different shapes, sizes, and ages. So even if you aren't picture perfect, you still can have a long and rewarding career as an actor.

You will also need flexibility in this business because each role can be entirely different from the last one. You have to be mentally prepared to "become" another person. That's called stretching, and you'll have to be able to stretch your talent into a variety of roles. If you are working another job to support yourself, you may need to arrange for flexible hours, too, in case you have to rehearse at odd hours.

You may not only have to work at night, but you also may be part of a traveling company, which requires a great deal of stamina and an ability to adapt to different circumstances. Most movies are now usually shot on location rather than on the back lot of a Hollywood studio. Shooting movies also demands working unusual hours under sometimes adverse conditions in all different climates. So be sure you really love to act before you think about becoming a star.

How to Find Work

Most actors work through a manager or agent who helps guide their careers and find jobs for them—for a fee, of course. You will have to have a portrait or head shot of yourself before you can even approach an agent. These shots should be taken by a professional photographer and should have a copy of your resume attached to the back.

On your resume, be sure to include your name, address, and phone number. But unlike most resumes, also include your height, weight, eye and hair color, and voice range (tenor, soprano, mezzo). Memberships in professional organizations should also be listed, as well as your theater and movie experience, training and education, special skills (dialects, foreign languages), sports, and dancing skills.

Professional actors are usually members of the Actors' Equity Association, a labor union for stage actors. You can become a member by signing an Equity contract, through its membership candidate program, or through its open-door admissions policy. Since so many of the members may be temporarily unemployed at any time, the dues are kept comparatively low. Other unions that help negotiate contracts and set salaries and working conditions are the Screen Actors Guild (SAG), the Screen Extras Guild (SEG), and the American Federation of Television and Radio Artists (AFTRA). Members of SAG and SEG work in the movies, films, television, and commercials; AFTRA members work in radio and television.

Training and Education

Now that you have seen that there is no guarantee for success or stardom simply by becoming an actor, and you still want to take the chance, let's take a look at some possible avenues to that stage door or movie camera. Maybe you will join the lucky 15 percent whom we refer to as working actors.

Starting in high school, or even earlier, get involved in school plays. See if you really like to memorize lines, follow stage directions, display emotions in public, and accept audience reaction to your performance, whether good or bad. It will get you ready for the real critics down the road.

Work with your drama and debate clubs and take speech and English classes, especially literature courses. It is important to begin observing people and how they react to life's situations. Now is the time to become aware of what motivates people to act and react as they do. You could also study different types of people, just in case you have to portray such a person on stage.

This is also a time for you to read all kinds of plays and attend live performances, if possible. You do not have to confine yourself to British and American plays. Many excellent plays have been translated into English from foreign languages all over the world, allowing you to see life and people from different cultural perspectives. Put yourself into different characters' shoes to determine what makes them tick.

Then, by the time you get to college, you will want to major in theater arts. Your course work will probably include a basic liberal arts curriculum with emphasis on the playwright's craft, production, design, and history of the theater, as well as drama and acting classes. Some people also take dancing and singing classes, especially if they want to perform in musicals.

You will also have to audition for roles. If you didn't get the role you wanted, work backstage. If there is a local community theater, audition there, too. In the summer, you might find a job in a summer stock company in resort towns or in some suburbs. There are also possibilities to hone your skills in dinner theaters in cities, suburbs, and rural areas.

You may choose to go to a school that specializes in training actors solely in the craft of acting. These are called dramatic arts schools and are located in most major cities. The best are probably located in New York and Los Angeles because these are the creative hubs of the United States. But since you do not need a college degree to be an actor, these schools might be the best choice for you. Just be sure to enroll in one with a good reputation.

Most major employers of actors are also located in New York and Los Angeles, and because of that, these are the most competitive cities for acting jobs in this country.

Forecast and Earnings

Chances are, you won't make a fortune as an actor, no matter how late you work or how talented you are. However, SAG and AFTRA members recently negotiated a contract that guaranteed movie and TV actors with speaking parts a minimum rate of $636 per day and $2,206 per five-day week.

Equity reports that the minimum weekly wage for Broadway actors is $1,252. So you can see that just because big Hollywood stars can command millions of dollars per picture, that is not what most actors earn in a lifetime.

Even though you have always wanted to be a star, you have to realize that stardom doesn't come easily, and sometimes it doesn't come at all, even to the most talented people. Sometimes luck plays a major part in a person's career. Sometimes the "look" can make or break your career. If you are not flexible enough to seek other roles that are suited to you, you may have difficulty landing the roles you want. If you persevere, have faith in your talent, and are willing to be patient and flexible, you can be counted as a working actor—if not an out-and-out star.

· · · · · · · · · · · · · · · · · ·

Directors

If you become an actor, you will work with a director. But what do directors do? Do you really need them? As much as you might think that an actor has to be the only one who can adequately interpret a role, directors see and interpret the whole play with all its characters, situations, and emotions. Therefore, they are in charge of selecting the cast, calling rehearsal times, and leading the cast and crew through to the final production.

Directors must oversee the whole production and even approve all costumes, set design, and music. They may have to soothe an actor's ego when their directions clash with the actor's interpretation of the role.

They also have to work under the stress of a budget and schedule and are responsible for all personnel problems. Each actor has to develop an individual role, and all actors have to be able to work as team members in order for the production to run smoothly.

Education and Training

Directors undergo intensive training, with the path to the theater being very similar to the path for actors. That is, the director should have a broad liberal arts background, with concentration in drama, directing, writing plays, stage movement, speech, and history of the theater. Business courses are also helpful.

How to Begin

You may start out at small, local theaters, and, as your reputation grows, you could advance to larger productions in major cities. You may work in movies and television, as well as in the theater.

Forecast and Earnings

Because of the demand for American productions throughout the world and the increase in the number of cable television stations, career prospects look good for directors, as well as for actors. The crossover between media and entertainment will contribute to new and more numerous career possibilities. And since people continue to attend the theater—and if you prefer live performance—you can also have a good career as a director in the theater. Recent salary reports indicate that the median annual salary for directors was $41,030.

Profile of an Actor/Director/Playwright

The word *starstruck* can truly describe Brian Kirst, an actor, director, and playwright. The acting bug hit Brian early—at about three or four years old. He grew up in a small town in Amish country in upstate New York. He was hooked when he saw *The Wizard of Oz* on a tiny black-and-white TV. He was a shy, sensitive little boy, and he fell in love with the fantasy. He also related to Dorothy, the shy heroine who overcame so many obstacles and survived. There were also some very scary elements in the movie, like the witches and flying monkeys, that started his lifelong attraction to horror movies. The movie was a good mix of reality and horror that appealed to Brian even at that young age. And he knew then that the theater was the life for him.

Brian's father had a love of the theater, directing plays in high school and performing in community theater, and Brian thinks he also inherited some artistic talent from his father's father and aunt. The paternal side of his family has also been involved in education and journalism.

Since he lived in such a small town, he watched more television than movies. The movie houses were just too far away to attend on a regular basis. His mother loved soap operas, so when he came home from preschool, he often watched them with his mother. He loved the daily dose of drama that he experienced even before he attended kindergarten. He even fell in love with some of the characters.

In second grade, his father drove him to a community theater where he appeared in his first show. It was given in a barn theater and started up as a summer stock company. The company only put on two shows and folded, but Brian did appear in *American Primitive* as John Quincy Adams, reading a letter that Adams had written to his father. Brian was the only one who memorized his lines—the other actors read the letters.

He loved the attention of the audience and older actors but never minded the rehearsals or memorizing the lines. At one point in the play, Brian was supposed to be sad enough to cry. He ingeniously thought of the idea of looking up into the bright lights to make him look sad. Since Brian spent many of his early years in period pieces, he thinks his biography should be titled *My Life in Knickers.*

His father also enjoyed teaching him songs and dance steps in an effort to build self-confidence, which his father had lacked in his youth. Although Brian would not call his father a "stage father," he did feel pressure to succeed. He was sometimes uncomfortable at auditions because of the pressure. He never had stage fright, as such, but he did have to learn to relax onstage and become more sure of himself. He now feels that he looks comfortable onstage.

He continued to perform in community theater productions and started to audition for professional actors' training. He eventually landed at the Chautauqua Institute during his sophomore year in high school. He had to drive to Cleveland for the audition to be accepted into the program. There he studied drama, music, combat, dance, movement, diction, voice, and improv during the summer.

For the program, Brian auditioned for Michael Kahn, who now runs the Shakespeare Theater in Washington, D.C. Brian wanted to move to New York City after graduation, but Kahn advised him to go to college and learn about life, study literature and history, and interact with other students. A well-rounded education is important, not only for acting, but also to provide a backup career.

Brian had the choice of attending a college, university, or conservatory to pursue his passion. He thinks people should pick a place where they are comfortable. Conservatories require a potential student to audition, usually with a prepared monologue, which could be comic or dramatic. He was rejected by one conservatory (not uncommon in the theater) but was accepted at another—the Theater School of De Paul University in Chicago.

He intended to complete a four-year program, but he was not asked back after his second year after a faculty review of his progress. He really wasn't happy there, partly because he came literally right from the farm, with no real-life experience, to a school that teaches a certain acting style. His insecurity and lack of life experience were definitely against him in that setting.

He then transferred to Columbia College, where he had one teacher per semester for class. With the combination of both schools, Brian achieved his bachelor's degree in fine arts, which included basic college courses where the students had to bring something of their major into other courses; for example, he wrote and directed pieces for history of disaster classes and composed a poem suite for math classes. It was then that he started to be interested in taking directing classes.

Brian recommends taking college prep courses in high school, with emphasis on English, literature, and debate. But most important is to be yourself and like yourself. Take time to develop other interests, such as sports, travel, or art. Learn about other people and their cultures, observe people in real life, and apply those experiences to your acting career.

By the time Brian finished high school, he had appeared in thirty shows; during college, he appeared in fifteen more. As a result, he had tired of auditioning. Writing plays became his next passion. As a senior at Columbia, he had written a play about child abuse called *Perished,* which was produced at the Director's Fest at Bailiwick Theater. It got good reviews in local newspapers and magazines, and Brian worked on it more, but he couldn't get it produced professionally.

So he founded his own theater company—Theatre Wyrzuc, Polish for "to throw out," specializing in throwing out women's and children's issues, pain, and abuse. Why women and children? Remember Brian's fascination for soap operas and *The Wizard of Oz?* And his admiration for people who survived great obstacles? His mother was also very emotional and shared many of her emotions with him. As a result, Brian feels more in tune with women's problems. Put all that together with the fact that Brian also experienced some abusive situations as a child, and his sensitivity to these issues can be easily understood.

As head of his own theater company, Brian wrote, directed, and produced plays, but he began more and more to perform those activities at Bailiwick, where he also became an artistic associate. He still uses his theater company for festivals and special events. At Bailiwick, Brian feels he really found his rhythm and style as a director. He loves to incorporate language and movement in his work and feels it is very vital to find an artistic home like Bailiwick. Bailiwick's artistic director, David Zak, allowed Brian to develop his skills and grow as an artist.

Brian, like most actors, directors, and writers, often has to take on a day job and work in the theater in the evenings for auditions, rehearsals, set design, wardrobe, and all the many tasks associated with getting a play on stage. Many actors wait on tables, tend bars, or work in retail, but when the economy is not good, people tend not to go to the theater or eat out as much. It's important for theater people to cultivate skills that can be transferred to other jobs, such as computers or training. The more skills you have, the better your chances of earning a living during the lean times.

Brian says that both acting and directing are strenuous, and you have to be flexible and resilient to survive. You should behave like a professional—know your lines, be ready for rehearsals, and steel yourself for rejection. Rejection is a given in the theater, and you should probably develop a support system to help you deal with it. His best advice is to like yourself, keep healthy, stay focused, and, above all, pursue your career with all your heart and soul.

· · · · · · · · · · · · · · · · ·

Dancers

Some of the most spectacular performing artists are dancers. Everyone loves to watch them. Whether it is ballet, modern, jazz, folk, or dances performed in musicals, operettas, or operas, these professionals dazzle us with fancy footwork, spectacular costumes, and incredible leaps, pirouettes, whirls, and twirls.

Whether they dance solo or with a group, dancers often leave us breathless with the power and grace of their movements and a seemingly effortless defiance of gravity. This must be the closest thing to flying with the birds that most humans ever achieve. And how beautiful it is to watch!

Training and Education

What does it take to fly with the birds? Or just to leap with grace and precision? Most dancers have to start training when they are still children. Girls can begin formal ballet training between eight and twelve years of age; boys can begin this training between twelve and sixteen years old. All dancers—including modern, jazz, and tap—should learn basic ballet techniques. Be sure to attend a good dance school, which you can find through its reputation in your community and publications focused on dance.

By the time you are a teenager, your dance teacher will know whether you have the body type and the potential to continue with the kind of intensive training that would lead to a professional dance career. If you are training for the ballet, this would be the time to begin concentrated training at a ballet school. Some of the major dance school companies may offer summer programs that could lead to your being admitted to their year-round training programs.

The key to success in ballet is practice, practice, practice—that is what you should be doing in your early and midteen years. In your late teens, you will begin your first professional auditions.

Other dancers have to be just as dedicated as ballet dancers. Their bodies and minds have to be disciplined; they must train, practice, and audition just like ballet dancers. Their training may not last as long as that for ballet dancers, however.

A career in dance does not necessarily require a college degree. In fact, because of all the time you must devote to training and practice, your academic life after high school may be a little sporadic. Still, some specialists recommend that you receive as broad an education as possible.

One thing you might want to keep in mind is that your career as a dancer may only last twelve to fifteen years. Therefore, you may want to think about preparing for a second career while you are still young. That may include getting a four-year degree that would allow you to become a dance teacher or choreographer when your active career as a dancer comes to an end.

Some colleges and universities do offer degrees in dance. If you decide not to attend the full four years, however, courses in music, literature, history of dance, and even acting could be helpful to your career. A dancer, after all, has to interpret roles much as an actor does. Feelings, emotions, and ideas are transmitted to the audience through body movements and facial expressions, and they all have to blend together with the music.

What It Takes

As you might suspect, dancers have to be in top physical form. They also have to be agile, coordinated, creative, persevering, and disciplined. Dancers, like actors, have to audition and, therefore, will often face rejection. Like actors, they also have to follow directions, rehearse long hours, and usually work within a troupe of other dancers. Dancers may also have to face the very real possibility of not being employed all the time. A backup job is often needed while you establish your career as a dancer, just as it is for actors.

How to Find Work

When you are ready to audition, check out the listings in dance-related magazines. After you are a bit more established in your career, word of mouth seems to be an effective method for getting auditions.

Another similarity between actors and dancers is that dancers also belong to unions. The American Guild of Musical Artists (AGMA) is the union for ballet, opera, and modern dancers. The American Federation of Television and Radio Artists (AFTRA) is for you if you work in those media. The Screen Actors Guild (SAG) and Screen Extras Guild (SEG) will be your movie unions, and Actors' Equity Association is for dancers who work in musical comedies.

How hard is it to become a working dancer? In some ways, it depends on how dedicated you are to your training and practice. Luck also plays a part in your career because in all the performing arts, the competition for jobs is high. There are always more people auditioning for any performance than there are roles to fill. And since the major hubs for these jobs are New York City and Hollywood, most artists flock there, and the competition for jobs becomes even more intense.

This is where your perseverance and faith in yourself become crucial. Remember that not everyone becomes a Barishnikov or an Astaire, but you can develop, with patience and practice, a good night-owl career in dance.

Another similarity with actors is that your initial salary may not be big because you may not work steadily as a dancer. You will probably have to supplement your dancing by working as an office temp, waiting on tables, or finding a dance-related job, if possible.

Forecast and Earnings

Your union will negotiate your contract with the producer of the show. Your contract may provide paid sick leave and vacations and possibly some health insurance. The median annual salary for dancers in 2000 was $22,470. So even though your salary may not fly with the birds, your dedication to your art, whether you are a ballet, modern, jazz, or tap dancer, will allow you to reach your own personal heights. Training, practice, and patience will be your guides in this dazzling night-owl career.

Musicians

Perhaps you feel you lack acting or dancing talent but would love to be performing on the stage, in the movies, or on television. You're taking piano, guitar, saxophone, or voice lessons, and your teacher thinks you have the real talent, natural rhythm, and dedication needed for a professional career. You find yourself loving to practice even though all your friends are out playing baseball or going to the movies. You have a great stereo and lots of CDs that you listen to for hours on end. You go to live concerts whenever possible and belong to your school band, have your own combo, or belong to the glee club.

In other words, maybe you can see yourself as a musician or singer up there on that stage, instead of as an actor or dancer. Or possibly you can see yourself conducting an orchestra in some beautiful concert hall in a glamorous European capital.

Well, you are on the right track already because of your lessons, your talent, and your practice. These are just the first few, but very important, steps. Budding musicians, just like all new actors and dancers, should know that career opportunities are limited and that only those talented people with perseverance and stamina will make it.

What are those opportunities? Musical career opportunities exist in chamber and classical music, folk, rock, pop, and jazz; in combos, trios, and orchestras; in choirs or as solo artists. You could be working in a studio, in a club, at the opera or ballet, in a musical comedy, or in a concert hall. You could perform in the movies, on television, or on the radio. Or you could be on tour throughout the world.

The three major categories of musical careers for night owls are instrumentalist, vocalist or singer, and conductor. Let's see which category you might fit into. It may also be possible to pursue a combination of two or even three of these categories. In other words, you might sing and play an instrument.

Instrumentalists are those who play musical instruments and perform solo or with a band, orchestra, or smaller group. You could play any instrument, from piano to cello, from drum to trumpet, or from saxophone to flute—and all instruments in between. Large musical groups, such as orchestras, need the full complement of string, wind, percussion, and brass, while a jazz combo may only need a pianist, drummer, and saxophonist.

Singers come in several categories: soprano, mezzo-soprano, contralto, tenor, baritone, and bass. Sopranos and tenors are at the higher end of the voice range, with the contralto and bass as the lowest. Mezzo-sopranos and baritones are middle-range voices. Your voice range may help you to determine where you will find your career niche. Your personal preference for music will do the rest. This preference will range anywhere from opera to folk, rock to rhythm and blues, country to rap, and all points in between.

Singers may work with a group in a musical comedy or operetta or interpret favorite songs in a personal style as a soloist. It is also possible to cross over successfully from one category of song to another. For example, opera stars such as José Carreras or Plácido Domingo have performed and recorded songs from the Broadway stage or folk songs native to their own countries. Broadway show tunes or romantic ballads can also be interpreted by a jazz instrumentalist or singer to put a whole new twist on them.

Conductors work with orchestras and bands by selecting the musicians and directing all their rehearsals and performances. These professionals must have the ability not only to interpret a whole piece, but also to lead the orchestra through every detail of that interpretation.

Conductors must be diplomatic because individual musicians may have different ideas about interpretation. Most successful conductors also have a dramatic style and stage presence that help them make a mark on the musical world.

Training and Education

For all these careers, you do not necessarily need a college degree, but you need the equivalent in training. You can get that training by studying privately with a master musician, at a conservatory of music, or through regular practice with a band or combo. Colleges and universities also offer degrees in music. So if you are taking music or singing lessons, you are off to the right start. For all these careers, you will, however, need a high school diploma.

What It Takes

As an instrumentalist, you have to be able to work well with others and be willing to study continually as well as practice. You will need all this in addition to talent and skill. On top of that, you have to be able to sight-read, transpose, and improvise music; specialize in at least one instrument; be able to play with other musicians; and be knowledgeable in the literature about your instrument.

Ideally, by the time you have graduated from high school, you will have learned how to read music and will have participated in some kind of performance to get used to being on the stage and to prepare yourself for auditions. You might also have performed solo by this time, as well as with the high school band or orchestra or with a small combo.

Singers also need raw talent, but they must develop specialized skills depending on the type of songs they choose to sing. For a successful career, it is essential to know English and all its nuances and, for many singers, a foreign language. You must also be able to sight-read, interpret, and memorize. Some piano-playing ability is also an asset. You will have to have some knowledge of vocal literature, be willing to continually study and practice, and have a touch of the performer in you to dramatically interpret an individual song or an entire opera.

Ideally, by the time you have finished high school, you will be able to play rudimentary piano, read music, and have some experience in performing alone or with a group. If your school has a glee club or your church has a choir, join them. The more you sing, the better you will become. And although some singers have been successful without any formal training, you are encouraged to keep up your formal training, especially if you are training for the opera, operetta, or stage shows.

Forecast and Earnings

Salaries for rock and jazz groups are too wide-ranging to estimate or average. Obviously, the bigger the name, the bigger the paycheck, so until you're a Britney Spears, you will definitely work irregularly and for lower fees.

In 2000, $36,740 was the average salary of musicians and singers. Salaries of members of major orchestras range from $24,720 to $100,196.

How to Find Work

The American Federation of Musicians of the United States and Canada (AFM), the world's largest union for performing artists, has some tips for aspiring musicians on how to break into the business. This group knows that you have invested a great deal of time and money in lessons, instruments, and maybe even costumes and stage equipment. Now you want to pursue a career with your talent.

According to AFM, you have to start out by talking to people who are already in the business. Find out where the jobs are, how musicians are treated at certain clubs or lounges, and who are the best agents and managers. These agents and managers are responsible for promoting you and eventually getting you jobs—or gigs, as they're called in the music world.

Because the music business is growing rapidly, there are a lot of people competing for the same jobs. The big jobs are again in New York and Los Angeles, as well as other major cities. For country music, you might head for Nashville or Branson. Dixieland jazz is at its best in New Orleans, and small jazz and rock clubs are found everywhere.

It is important for beginning musicians to protect themselves from unethical agents and managers. For this reason, musicians as well as actors and dancers often join unions or professional membership organizations. They include AFM, AGMA, and the American Symphony Orchestra League. The National Association for Music Education is the accrediting association for postsecondary musical education programs, and it supplies career information. All these organizations are set up to guide, protect, and encourage professional musicians through a long and rewarding career in the musical field of their choice. And, as we all know, life without music is no life at all.

Profile of a Musician

John Brumbach, jazz saxophonist, did not exactly come from a musical family, although his father dabbled with the piano, and his mother loved records of Frank Sinatra and Broadway musicals, such as *Oklahoma* and *My Fair Lady*. John himself started taking piano lessons when he was about eight years old, but he characterizes his teacher as a "third-rate hack." He played for weddings and graduation parties in hotels and, according to John, didn't "know where it was at" with music. He also took clarinet lessons for about a year but couldn't wait to get out of that class.

During his high school years, John didn't pursue music very seriously, but he remembers loving Elvis Presley and his sound. He also had a brief fling with a rhythm and blues band in his basement. All in all, his musical background at this stage did not point to his later success with the saxophone.

During high school, John ran into a recurring problem in his life that he eventually overcame and which may have actually led him back to his real addiction: music. That problem was drug and alcohol abuse. The problem followed him for years, in and out of musical attempts and actual successful career opportunities. John wants to make it clear to any aspiring musician that the demon was within him—it had nothing to do with pursuing a musical career or associating with musicians. In fact, the musicians he plays with now lead clean and sober lives, and that helps him to keep on the straight and narrow path, too.

It took John a few years to realize what his true path in life was. In college, he experienced severe problems from the drug abuse. He became paranoid and nervous all the time. Unfortunately, by his second or third semester in college, John was incapable of doing academic work. He was very good at math and found it easy and enjoyable, but by that time nothing worked for him.

Somehow, almost intuitively, John knew that music could act in a therapeutic way for him. He dropped out of the University of Illinois, borrowed some money from his brother to buy a horn, and started to hang out with musicians. At that time, he loved listening to records of the soulful sax soloist King Curtis and the Queen of Soul, Aretha Franklin.

John also picked up some exercise books and just started playing intensely. He admits that the only time he felt okay was when he was playing. He was living in a rooming house and playing about eight hours a day. This was his training for becoming a successful professional jazz saxophonist. Just as a writer has to write, and a dancer has to dance, a musician has to play—and sometimes that intensive playing becomes the musician's formal education.

During that time, John was playing the blues with his brother, and he truly thought he had found the answer for his life and the solution to his problems: music. But his addictions came back to haunt him again in Los Angeles, where he was beginning to explore new career possibilities. He lost his career and his wife there, as a result of drug and alcohol abuse, and decided to return to Chicago.

After about two years playing in honky-tonks, John had the good fortune to start playing with master jazz pianist Erwin Helfer at Andy's, a jazz institution in Chicago. John, a talented man in two fields, had been working during the day as an engineer. That job was beginning to stress him out, and he was also realizing how important music was to him. It was time to make a decision that would affect him and his family for the rest of his life.

John decided to return full-time to music, both performing and teaching. But his engineering company offered him part-time work, which he accepted. This has worked out well for John, who now works one to two days a week as an engineer, which allows him to make a full-time commitment to music.

His private students range in age from nine to forty years old, although he did once have a sixty-five-year-old student. He currently teaches eight adults and four children.

Even with the part-time engineering job and the private tutorials, John still has time to practice. He has built a soundproof practice room in his attic for that purpose. This is what he calls his "woodshedding" time—the time when he practices alone.

John is a firm believer in practice; he thinks it makes a musician grow. Through practice, he stays excited and committed and continues to learn about himself. But he thinks that teaching music helps him to articulate what he knows intuitively.

John admits that there was a time in his life when he downplayed the technical aspect of his art. He now knows that it is extremely important and leads to more creative aspects of playing. The ease of performing comes from knowing the technical aspects of the music and your instrument so well that all the time and effort you put into it will pay off in the performance itself.

In performance, John says, you will hardly know that you have a horn in your hand. All your musical expression will go "from the center of your being out into the center of the universe." John thinks that when you are playing with inspired and sensitive musicians, it is a spiritual and mental experience, an act of selflessness. For John, it is the greatest "high" he will ever want to achieve. That is when his technical and creative skills merge into an experience far more powerful than drugs. John is happy to be doing what he is doing and plans to be a musician for a long time.

Since John works at night, however, he admits it's hard on family life. His wife works normal hours, but he does have her support for his career choice. He loves not having to fight rush-hour traffic, and shopping is easier during the day. He also enjoys conversing with his regular customers at Andy's, and he feels that he's a more valuable employee because he knows them.

John advises anyone who wants to be a professional musician to first of all follow your heart. He emphasizes that you have to look out for yourself financially, but he cautions against going into music for the money. He thinks you should find positive and creative people, especially teachers, and avoid hacks. Musicians should be musicians out of love, pure and simple. Seek out others who are passionate about music as early as you can.

John also thinks that, although you really don't have to go to college to be a musician, education enhances everyone's life. It doesn't hurt to take business courses in college as well as music because you will have to negotiate contracts, work with agents, and manage your money. You should also play as often as possible, even if it's in your basement or garage, alone or with a group. Be with musicians, learn from them, and play with them. That way, you'll have the beginnings of a truly rewarding career with music, no matter what the hours are.

Behind the Scenes

Not all the people in the entertainment industry are visible, but they are absolutely necessary to our enjoyment of the various performers. These are the stagehands, carpenters, makeup artists, hairstylists, costumers, electricians, set designers, and property handlers.

Among the night owls who are not in the movies but who bring them to us are box office attendants and concession managers. You may want to make a career of these jobs, or you may be able to take these jobs as you pursue your dancing, acting, or musical careers.

Concession attendants work at night to be sure that we have enough food and beverages to get us through the performance. At movie theaters, attendants serve food and beverages shortly before the movie begins, but for stage performances and the opera, food and beverages are consumed during the intermissions.

Concession attendants assist in stocking supplies, maintaining the work area, operating cooking and popping machines, and sometimes hauling bulk-food items from storage to the work area.

Box office attendants sell tickets, answer customer questions about performance times and prices, and describe show content, if necessary. They also help the manager count cash and keep records. Sometimes they double as doorkeepers or ushers.

Theater managers, ushers, and doorkeepers round out the night owls who open the doors and keep the theaters and movie houses running smoothly so that we can enjoy the wonderful performances of the artists on stage or on film.

For Further Information

You'll find a wealth of information online at these organizations' websites. You can also write to them directly to obtain publications and additional information about entertainment careers.

Actors' Equity Association
165 West Forty-Sixth Street
New York, NY 10036
www.actorsequity.org

American Arts Alliance
805 Fifteenth Street NW
Washington, DC 20004
www.americanartsalliance.org

American Dance Guild
P.O. Box 2006
New York, NY 10021
www.americandanceguild.org

American Federation of Musicians of the United States and
   Canada
Paramount Building
1501 Broadway, Suite 600
New York, NY 10036
www.afm.org

American Federation of Television and Radio Artists
4340 East-West Highway, Suite 204
Bethesda, MD 20814
www.aftra.org

American Guild of Musical Artists
1727 Broadway
New York, NY 10019

American Guild of Organists
475 Riverside Drive, Suite 1260
New York, NY 10015
www.agohq.org

American Music Conference
5790 Armada Drive
Carlsbad, CA 92008
www.amc-music.com

American Symphony Orchestra League
33 West Sixtieth Street, Fifth Floor
New York, NY 10023
www.symphony.org

Americans for the Arts
1000 Vermont Avenue NW, Twelfth Floor
Washington, DC 20005
www.artsusa.org

Associated Actors and Artists of America
165 West Forty-Sixth Street, Suite 500
New York, NY 10036

Association for Theatre in Higher Education
P.O. Box 4537
Boulder, CO 80306
www.athe.org

Association of Performing Arts Presenters
1112 Sixteenth Street NW, Suite 400
Washington, DC 20036
www.artspresenters.org

Bailiwick Arts Center
1229 West Belmont
Chicago, IL 60657
www.bailiwick.org

Broadcast Music, Inc.
320 West Fifty-Seventh Street
New York, NY 10019
www.bmi.com

Canadian Actors' Equity Association
National Office
44 Victoria Street, Twelfth Floor
Toronto, ON M5C 3C4
Canada

Canadian Actors' Equity Association
Western Office
505 Hudson House
321 Water Street
Vancouver, BC V6B 1B8
Canada
www.cala.com

The College Music Society
202 West Spruce
Missoula, MT 59802
www.music.org

Conductors Guild, Inc.
c/o North Lakeside Cultural Center
6219 North Sheridan Road
Chicago, IL 60660
www.conductorsguild.org

Dance/USA
1156 Fifteenth Street, Suite 820
Washington, DC 20005
www.danceusa.org

International Alliance of Theatrical Stage Employees, Motion
    Picture Technicians, Artists, and Allied Crafts of the United
    States, Its Territories, and Canada, AFL-CIO, CLC
1430 Broadway, Twentieth Floor
New York, NY 10018
www.iatse.lm.com

John F. Kennedy Center for the Performing Arts
Internship Coordinator
Alliance for Arts Education
2700 F Street NW
Washington, DC 20566
www.kennedy-center.org

Music Teachers National Association
441 Vine Street, Suite 505
Cincinnati, OH 45202
www.mtna.org

National Association for Music Education (MENC)
1806 Robert Fulton Drive
Reston, VA 20191
www.menc.org

National Association of Schools of Music (NASM)
11250 Roger Bacon Drive, Suite 21
Reston, VA 20190
www.arts-accredit.org

National Association of Theatre Owners
4605 Lankershim Boulevard, Suite 340
North Hollywood, CA 91602
www.natoonline.org

National Endowment for the Arts
1100 Pennsylvania Avenue NW
Washington, DC 20506
www.arts.endow.gov

The National Music Council
425 Park Street
Upper Montclaire, NJ 07043
www.musiccouncil.org

Screen Actors Guild
5757 Wilshire Boulevard
Los Angeles, CA 90036
www.sag.org

CHAPTER SEVEN

Keeping Us out of Harm's Way

Night Owls Who Serve the Public

Since September 11, 2001, our nation has realized more than ever how important some careers are to our safety and security. New heroes emerged from the rubble of the World Trade Center in New York, men and women who worked tirelessly to rescue and recover, clean up, and in many cases, give their own lives to help others. Before then, most of us probably took firefighters and police officers for granted. Now a whole network of agencies has been formed to coordinate homeland security and to prevent further acts of terrorism.

Because of the attacks, security guards have also become more important to our everyday lives, since buildings have become possible targets of terrorism. Social workers also work to ensure our emotional security, especially during times of crisis and emergency. And we can't forget the dispatcher who makes sure that the vital emergency services are delivered in a timely fashion. Still others help us get through the night by providing counseling in cases of drug abuse, domestic violence, or runaway children. Without these dedicated professionals, our lives would be without the safety net that we all need when we are in trouble.

Law Enforcement Officers

Most of us see police officers every day on the way to school or work. They may be patrolling the streets in cars, on foot, on a motorcycle, or on a horse. They could be directing traffic at busy intersections or chasing a car down the street with sirens blaring and lights flashing.

They may even be pulling us over to give us a ticket for speeding. Unfortunately, they may also have arrived at the parking meter a minute before we do and be writing a parking ticket for us. Sometimes we might have to call them for help with prowlers or burglars. We may also see them at the scene of a fire, accident, or expressway tie-up.

Law enforcement officers also work behind the scene. There are, for example, detectives, special agents, and experts in chemical analysis and fingerprint identification. In smaller towns, where there is no official police department, we might find town or county sheriffs. In addition, every state has its own police squad, also called state troopers.

The federal government has a special investigative department known as the Federal Bureau of Investigation, more commonly called the FBI. Still other federal law enforcement agents work for the Department of Treasury, while Secret Service agents protect the president and other top federal officials and their families.

Law enforcement personnel are just as concerned with the prevention of crime as they are with solving crimes and arresting the criminals. Municipal police officers are becoming more and more involved in community work and are trying to be more responsive to the needs of the particular community. In some cases, drugs and gangs are the biggest problem. In other communities, burglaries and petty larceny need the most attention. An effective police department is aware of the specific problems and population it is dealing with.

Detectives aren't as noticeable as the "cops on the beat" because they work in civilian clothes, but they are there helping investigate crimes, gather evidence, and conduct on-site interviews with victims and witnesses to crime.

Agents in the FBI are charged with investigating specific federal crimes, including organized crime, espionage, kidnapping, sabotage, and terrorism. They may also specialize in such financial crimes as embezzlement or counterfeiting. Other federal agents work for the U.S. Customs Service and the Internal Revenue Service.

State troopers are found mainly on intrastate highways, patrolling for lawbreakers and assisting drivers in trouble. They also are found at accident or disaster scenes, where they clear traffic and see that victims are taken care of. If you ever have car trouble on the highway, they will be there to give you assistance. Sometimes state troopers are called upon to help solve crimes, especially where there is no local police department.

What It Takes

Wherever you work as a law enforcement officer, you have to have certain characteristics and personal qualities. You must be honest and responsible and have a real need to help people. Since you are involved on a daily basis with people in trouble or in stress, you have to be able to think quickly, demonstrate fairness, and exercise good judgment.

Special law enforcement officers are employed at colleges and universities, public transportation systems, or school districts. Or they may work for the federal government in the Immigration and Naturalization Service; the Drug Enforcement Agency; the Bureau of Alcohol, Tobacco, and Firearms; or as customs inspectors.

In many cases, before you become a law enforcement officer or federal agent, you may have to be tested for your psychological stability, use of drugs, and honesty. You may be required to take a lie detector test and undergo a background check.

Training and Education

How do you get into law enforcement? Like many employers, police departments and law enforcement agencies want people with at least a high school diploma. More and more cities and states are, however, requiring some college work if not a degree from a college or university. Community colleges offer courses in law enforcement, but no matter where you attend, certain courses are recommended. These courses include English, American history, psychology, business law, and sociology.

Your communications skills, especially in English, are extremely important because you will have to write reports and verbally transmit directions to a wide variety of people to ensure their safety. You will also be called on occasionally to testify in court. Because Spanish is spoken by so many people in the United States, some knowledge of it is very helpful.

As a law enforcement officer, you have to be a U.S. citizen and at least twenty years old. In addition to your academic credentials, you have to be in prime physical condition because you must undergo strict physical examinations, including vision testing.

Before you become a police officer, you have to undergo certain training. The length of time varies from location to location but usually includes some classroom instruction that emphasizes constitutional and state law, civil ordinances, and civil rights laws. In addition, the training course covers self-defense, traffic control, and the use of firearms.

Where to Start

After your training as a police officer, you will probably start out on patrol. During this time, you will work with a more experienced officer in different areas of your beat. You will have to be on the lookout for anything unusual, suspicious, or dangerous. You might even have to respond to actual calls. You will keep in constant contact with headquarters throughout your shift.

After a certain period as a beat officer or patrol officer, which varies from department to department, you may be eligible for promotion, usually to detective. Or you may decide to specialize in a specific area, such as traffic or communications. In order to be promoted up the line, from sergeant to lieutenant to captain, you have to pass a written examination that will be evaluated with your performance to that point.

To apply for a job as an FBI agent, you need to have a college degree in accounting or be a law school graduate; have three years' full-time experience; and speak, read, and write in a foreign language fluently. You must be a U.S. citizen, be physically fit, and have good, though perhaps corrected, vision. If you are accepted, you receive your training at the FBI academy in Virginia.

If you want to work for the Treasury Department as a special agent, you need a college degree and at least three years of work experience, with two of them involving criminal investigation, or a combination of education and experience. If accepted, you then have to complete seventeen weeks of training.

Forecast and Earnings

Your job prospects are good in the next few years if you decide to become a law enforcement officer or special agent. Those who have bachelor's degrees or have received some college training will receive the best job offers. Salaries, benefits, and opportunities for advancement are quite good in this field, and many police officers can retire rather young and receive a good pension. Often you will also be able to earn overtime pay, and your benefits will probably include paid vacations and sick days, as well as medical and life insurance.

Salaries vary according to whether you are working for a city, state, or federal agency, or whether you work in a big city or small town.

What to Expect

Now, if you think that law enforcement work is for you, you have to realize that for many of the jobs you are on call twenty-four hours a day. You have to be prepared to work different shifts and to give up weekends and holidays.

Federal agents may have to travel with very little notice. But if you think you have what it takes, the night owl in you will overcome these obstacles.

Profile of a Campus Police Officer

Ron Ervin represents a certain kind of police officer. Working on a campus, he is very familiar with shift work. He has worked on a four-week rotating shift, which he likes pretty well. Every four weeks it changes from 7 A.M. to 3 P.M., 3 P.M. to 11 P.M., and 11 P.M. to 7 A.M. He feels this is a much easier schedule to adjust to than a one-week rotation, especially when it comes to eating and sleeping habits. He also has an easier time planning his weekends and vacations.

He developed his interest in law enforcement in the eighth grade, and it has never left him. Because he came from a broken home and then lost both his parents, he wanted to turn this pain into doing something worthwhile with his life.

Ron found encouragement from one of his teachers and also from some police officers he knew at the time. He even got involved in a local ride-along program, which allowed high school students to participate in certain police activities.

Ron graduated from high school when he was only seventeen, and no police department would hire him at that age. He then decided to join the U.S. Marine Corps for four years. And—you guessed it—he was an MP (military police). He received valuable on-the-job training and was in charge of his company's armory, which allowed him to learn a great deal about firearms.

When Ron left the service, he applied at Purdue University's North Central extension campus and was hired. At that time he received one year of basic training, including a ten-week course at the police academy. His time at the academy was devoted to studying criminal law, first aid, traffic accidents, domestic disputes, and riot control. Sometimes lifelike scenarios were set up by the more experienced officers to see how the cadets would react to them.

He thinks that the graveyard shift is difficult but challenging. He is the only officer on duty at that time, and he really likes that feeling of independence. Sometimes the campus is quiet, especially during the summer, when there are very few students. At about 4 A.M., he begins to get tired, and he has no one to talk to, except maybe the custodial staff in buildings he patrols. He often drinks a lot of coffee and depends on the radio for company.

Ron doesn't just patrol the campus, though. The campus police department has a mutual assistance program with the Hammond Police Department, so he patrols the immediate community, too. If he sees anything suspicious, such as a burglary in progress, he radios the Hammond police, who come and provide assistance. This whole program gives everyone on campus and in the surrounding community a better sense of security.

Some people whom he stops for a traffic offense or parking problem really don't believe that he is a genuine police officer because he works on campus. They think he is a security guard and only believe him when they meet in court.

Besides the independence he loves on the graveyard shift, Ron loves the challenge of knowing that no two calls are ever the same. Sometimes he's called for a family dispute, a barroom brawl, or a foot pursuit. Sometimes he redirects kids who are just out wandering after curfew.

On weekends, there are usually more alcohol-related incidents than on weeknights, especially right after the bars close. There is always more danger at night simply because you can't always see it coming. But Ron says that edge can make your blood run, and you are suddenly wide awake.

Ron thinks that it's a good idea to get an associate's degree if you want to become a police officer, but a bachelor's degree is even better. That degree will be a must for everyone in the near future. Typical courses to take are criminology, computer science, and English. If you take a foreign language, it should be Spanish.

Many police cars are now equipped with computers that allow officers to check license plates, drivers' licenses, stolen cars, or pending calls. This new technological capability seems to be effective in deterring crime because would-be criminals are becoming aware that patrol cars arrive on the scene much faster now.

Ron emphasizes grammar, spelling, writing, and verbal skills. You have to be able to talk to a wide variety of people, no matter which shift you're working. You will write up many official reports, which the judge and the defense and prosecuting attorneys have to read. These are legal documents and are also reflections on your department. If you are a poor speller, at least learn how to use your dictionary.

Ron suggests that you ask your local police department whether it sponsors ride-along programs for young people. Some state police departments also offer summer camps to familiarize students with police work. Get to know your local law enforcement officers. Talk to them about their jobs and see whether they might recommend books to read about the work.

Would Ron recommend this work? Without hesitation. It is very challenging, he says, and he is in a position to do something good for other people. That's what he has had in mind since eighth grade.

Firefighters

Another equally important career for those of you who are not only night owls but also want to help people in trouble is that of firefighter. These professionals not only put out fires, they also try to prevent fires from starting by inspecting buildings and their fire escapes and by checking for any dangerous and flammable materials on the premises. Firefighters also work with schools and community groups to instruct them on fire-prevention techniques, the use of smoke detectors, and how to react to a fire.

When a fire occurs, wherever it occurs, the firefighter's primary duty is to put it out quickly and efficiently and with as little damage or loss of life as possible. At the scene of the fire, they may have to perform a variety of duties, including giving first aid, operating heavy equipment, and working with emergency medical technicians (EMTs).

When they're not on the scene of a fire, they spend their time at the fire station, probably working more than the standard forty-hour workweek. At the station, they help maintain the equipment, write up reports, and sometimes attend training sessions. They need to keep up with current literature in the field. They sleep and eat at the station, too, because of the demands of shift rotations.

What to Expect

Firefighters work different shifts, generally more than forty hours a week. They may work a straight twenty-four hours and be off for forty-eight hours. Or they might work the day shift for a couple of weeks and then night shift for a couple of weeks. The shifts vary from place to place, and firefighters are on call at any time during the shift.

Fire fighting is dangerous, often grueling work. Firefighters are exposed to flames, smoke, hazardous chemicals, toppling buildings, and caved-in walls. They perform their work outdoors in all possible weather conditions. They assist in rescuing victims of tornadoes, hurricanes, floods, and other natural disasters, as well as human-caused accidents such as oil spills or chemical explosions.

Because firefighters work under pressure, they have to exercise good judgment in emergency situations, make immediate decisions to ensure safety, and be physically strong. A firefighter has to be able to wake up from a sound sleep and instantly be ready to respond to a dangerous situation.

As a member of a team that lives and works together, firefighters must be able to get along well with other people. This kind of teamwork demands reliability, flexibility, and a good sense of humor. So, if you're still interested in becoming a firefighter, let's look at what it will take.

Training and Education

To become a firefighter you need to be at least eighteen years old and have a high school diploma or its equivalent. Then you must pass a written exam, a medical exam, and various tests of physical strength, stamina, and coordination. A drug test may also be required. Those with the highest scores on all exams—and a negative drug test—are admitted to a training program. If you've served as an apprentice or intern at a fire department or have had experience as a volunteer firefighter, you will probably have a better chance of being a successful candidate.

Some fire departments have apprenticeship programs, and the National Fire Academy in Emmitsburg, Maryland, conducts training sessions. You can also take courses in some colleges and universities in fire engineering and fire science.

The training begins in class for a few weeks in such subjects as fire fighting techniques, building codes, fire prevention, and appropriate medical procedures. You learn how to use your equipment, including ladders, axes, and extinguishers. After the training period, you are finally assigned to your fire station. But you're still on probation, and you're really just beginning to learn.

Because of the increasing responsibilities of firefighters and the more sophisticated equipment and technology involved in fire fighting, firefighters must continually update their knowledge in techniques and procedures. This continuing education is especially necessary for promotion. Some firefighters receive training in disaster preparedness and control of hazardous materials.

Sometimes the department itself offers additional training programs for its employees, and some states also have such programs. If you decide to pursue further education, you probably want to take courses in management, budgeting, advanced equipment, writing, and public speaking.

Promotion within the department is possible after a few years. The usual progression is this: engineer, lieutenant, captain, battalion chief, assistant chief, deputy chief, all the way to chief. You have to pass a written exam to be considered for promotion. Then your superiors factor in your previous performance on the job and the number of years you have served. More and more fire departments also require advanced degrees for promotion to chief.

Like police officers, firefighters receive good pay, benefits, and pension plans. Overtime is available, and most departments provide protective clothing and dress uniforms.

Forecast and Earnings

Firefighters may find entry-level employment possibilities in smaller communities that need more full-time firefighters to supplement the volunteer force. High job turnover is unusual in fire fighting, so competition for jobs may be intense. In 2000, the median hourly wage for firefighters was $16.43.

Security Guards

If fire fighting and law enforcement are not your choices for keeping people safe, perhaps you would like to become a security guard. These people keep watch over our offices, department stores, banks, and hospitals through patrols and inspections of property. They watch for things like fire, suspicious activity, and vandalism. They often work with department store detectives to catch customers or employees stealing merchandise.

Or you might be assigned to a museum, a laboratory, or a military base where you would guard art objects, formulas, or secret files. Parks and sports facilities also hire guards to check incoming and outgoing personnel and vehicles. They assist customers by answering questions, giving directions, explaining the facilities, and directing traffic. Some people hire guards to protect them or their families from harm or kidnapping—hence the name bodyguard. Some guards also deliver large sums of money in armored cars from one place of business to another.

Depending on where you work, you patrol on foot, by car, or even on a motor scooter. You have to check out the offices, doors, and windows, as well as any unauthorized people in the building. You may even have to check the heating and sprinkler systems.

Sometimes you are able to check all this out from your workstation with the help of television monitors. This occurs when cameras are placed in strategic areas of the building so that they "patrol" for you.

And if you're not a clotheshorse, you won't mind wearing a uniform. Most guards wear uniforms, and they also carry flashlights and two-way radios. Sometimes they carry guns, though they rarely have to use them.

Many times, the work is routine, but guards have to be ready for anything. Very often, guards who work at night work alone. Many organizations now require guards twenty-four hours a day, seven days a week, every day of the year. In these cases, guards may work on rotating shifts. And, yes, guards have to work weekends and holidays.

What It Takes

How do you become a guard? To be licensed as a guard, as most states require, you have to be at least eighteen years old. In addition, you have to take some classroom training and pass a background check. It is also preferred that you have a high school diploma. If you have to drive a vehicle on patrol, you also need a valid driver's license. And if you have to carry a gun, you need a gun license.

If you have had previous military experience or were a police officer, you will be valuable to employers. And since law enforcement officers can retire fairly early, they often become guards after retirement. The varying shifts also attract people to guard work.

Whether you choose to be a security guard as a first or second career, you have to be in good health and have no police record. Your emotional life has to be stable, and you must be reliable, dependable, and physically fit. You may also be required to take lie detector and drug tests.

Training and Education

After you've been hired, you will probably receive on-the-job training. This training might include public relations, emergency procedures, report writing, and capture of suspected criminals. You might learn about firearms or more about the facility you will be guarding. You will also learn about electronic surveillance techniques.

If you want to advance in the security business, you may have to consider further education. For example, some related college courses may make administrative positions possible. If you have management skills, you may want to open your own business.

Forecast and Earnings

Because more businesses are concerned with security and there is relatively high turnover, there should be plenty of jobs available in this field through 2010. Salaries vary from region to region and from facility to facility, with the median annual salary being $17,570. The more experience you accumulate, the more you earn. Guards who are hired directly by individual organizations instead of through an agency usually earn more. They also usually get better benefits and have more job security.

....

Dispatchers

If security guard work is not for you, you might want to consider becoming a dispatcher. These are the people who receive calls for help and coordinate all services to solve the problem. Basically there are seven different types of dispatchers:

1. **Public safety dispatchers** work for police and fire departments and ambulance services. Generally they are part of the 911 system that takes emergency calls, asks pertinent questions regarding the nature of the emergency, finds out the location of the emergency, and decides on appropriate action. If it is a medical case, dispatchers keep talking to the caller in order to give any necessary first-aid advice or to find out exact details of the emergency. They

are also in contact with the paramedics to get updated information on the patient's condition.

2. **Truck dispatchers** work with drivers and customers to expedite delivery, assign drivers, and provide scheduling.

3. **Bus dispatchers** keep buses on schedule, both local and long distance.

4. **Train dispatchers** make sure trains arrive and depart on time.

5. **Taxi dispatchers** inform cab drivers when and where a cab is needed. They also keep records of any road service calls.

6. **Tow-truck dispatchers** are there for emergency road-service and make sure that a tow truck is sent to the site.

7. **Utility service dispatchers** send out emergency crews in case of electricity, gas, or water outages.

Training and Education

Most employers require a high school diploma. Some may also give you a test of basic language and math skills; others may test your strength and coordination and mechanical aptitude.

Part of each job entails keeping records, writing reports, and recording the actions taken in each situation. Sometimes entries are made directly into a computer. For all these jobs, oral and written communications skills must be very good, and because more and more computers are being used in dispatching, computer skills are essential.

Forecast and Earnings

The job outlook is fairly promising for dispatching because there is a rather high degree of turnover in this field. This can be a high-pressure job, and some people leave it after a few years.

Salaries for dispatchers vary too much even to quote them, based on the type and size of organization as well as geographic location. It is a good idea to join a union that will look out for working conditions, salaries, and other benefits.

Social Service Workers

Many people have to work at night to protect our mental and emotional security. These include caseworkers, drug and alcohol abuse counselors, and residential counselors. They work in group residences, halfway houses, mental health centers, hospitals, and social service agencies. They help runaway teenagers, battered women and children, and people with psychological problems that they cannot solve themselves.

Many of these professionals work primarily during the day, but they are always on call, including nights and weekends, especially in times of crisis. If they work in group homes, they usually work rotating shifts. Generally they work under the supervision of social workers or sometimes even psychologists.

These professionals provide a wide variety of services, including setting up day-care programs, teaching basic skills, leading recreational activities, and providing transportation to those who need it. They work under pressure because they work with people who have problems that have to be solved, sometimes very quickly.

Training and Education

The minimum requirement for being a social worker is a bachelor's degree in social work (B.S.W.). You may want to specialize in one or another aspect of social services, such as family problems, crisis intervention, drug counseling, or rehabilitation.

Or you may decide you want to work with the elderly, teenagers, or the developmentally disabled. You can continue your education and earn a master's degree in human services and social work to prepare for advancement in this field.

What It Takes

Social workers directly counsel their clients on a wide range of problems, including homelessness, illness, drug and alcohol abuse, and child or spouse abuse. They usually specialize in child welfare, family services, or mental health services, or they might specialize in school, community, or clinical social work. Often they have to schedule evening and weekend meetings with their clients, and some are on call at all hours.

All these professionals have to be extremely dedicated, patient, and sensitive to other people and their often severe problems. They have to be dependable and responsible as well as emotionally stable. The work is rewarding, especially when successfully solving problems, but since social workers are always dealing with troubled individuals or families, it can be very difficult work.

If you have your master's degree in social work (M.S.W.), you will be able to find work in health care, including mental health care facilities. If you decide to go into administrative or supervisory work, you also need an M.S.W. A doctorate of social work (D.S.W.) is needed for teaching and research positions.

Earnings

The salaries vary according to degree, specialization, and level of experience, but the average annual salary was $31,470 in 2000.

....

Keeping Us Safe

Social service workers at all levels are always needed because people are always in need. Police officers, firefighters, dispatchers, social service professionals—these hardworking professionals make our lives more secure. All these careers are necessary and worthwhile. You just have to want to help people, have the courage and stamina to do it, and get the education to prepare you for other possibilities as a public-service night owl.

....

For Further Information

For more information about careers in law enforcement, emergency services, security services, and social work, contact the following organizations.

American Train Dispatchers Department
Brotherhood of Locomotive Engineers
1370 Ontario Street
Cleveland, OH 44113
www.ble.org

Association of Public Safety Communications Officials
2040 South Ridgewood
South Daytona, FL 32119
www.acpointl.org

Association of Social Work Boards
400 South Ridge Parkway, Suite B
Culpeper, VA 22701
www.aswb.org

Council on Social Work Education
1725 Duke Street, Suite 500
Alexandria, VA 22314
www.cswe.org

International Association of Fire Fighters
1750 New York Avenue NW
Washington, DC 20006
www.iaff.org

National Academy of Emergency Medical Dispatch
139 East South Temple, Suite 530
Salt Lake City, UT 84111
www.naemd.org

National Association of Social Workers
750 First Street NE, Suite 700
Washington, DC 20002
www.socialworkers.org

National Fire Academy
Degrees at a Distance Program
16825 South Seton Avenue
Emmitsburg, MD 21727
www.usfa.fema.gov/nfa

U.S. Border Patrol
Chester A. Arthur Building
425 I Street NW
Washington, DC 20536
www.usborderpatrol.gov

U.S. Bureau of Alcohol, Tobacco, and Firearms
Personnel Division
650 Massachusetts Avenue NW, Room 4100
Washington, DC 20226
www.atf.treas.gov

U.S. Fire Administration
16825 South Seton Avenue
Emmitsburg, MD 21727
www.usfa.fema.gov

U.S. Secret Service
Personnel Division
950 H Street NW, Suite 7400
Washington, DC 20223
www.ustreas.gov/usss

CHAPTER EIGHT

Even More Careers for Night Owls

With our topsy-turvy, day-for-night world, it's good to know that certain other services are available to us twenty-four hours a day. When we run out of milk, baby formula, medicine, or gas in the middle of the night, we are almost always able to find an all-night convenience store or gas station.

To get our newspaper in the morning, we need people who are working the printing presses during the night. Even some professionals, such as teachers, have to work nights. So let's take a look at some of these career possibilities to see if there's a place for another night owl or two.

Salespeople

This country sometimes seems to be run by its salespeople—someone is always selling something somewhere. It may be in a department or grocery store, through the mail, on the radio or television, in magazines or newspapers. There are now even several shopping channels on television that run all day and all night, and computer online services allow you to shop on your home computer.

Sometimes we buy from farm stands or from flea markets, where everything imaginable can be bought and sold. Kids start selling lemonade at an early age, and entrepreneurs sell their own homemade products to local stores or individual customers. Luckily for all those salespeople, there are enough of us who love to shop till we drop.

Salespeople have to know their products well enough to inform customers about their special features. They are often responsible for ringing up the sales and packaging the items purchased. Most cash registers are now computerized, so sales personnel must learn that skill.

Those who work at night also often have to work holidays and weekends. Prompt, efficient service is important for night salespeople because the customer is eager to get home and go to bed.

What It Takes

Even though there are no formal educational requirements for sales, most employers do prefer a high school diploma or equivalent, unless, of course, it is a part-time job you work while attending high school. However, certain personal qualities are important for this work.

First of all, you should like dealing with people. This may require a combination of patience, good will, and a healthy sense of humor. Second, your appearance is important because you sometimes serve as the only store representative the customer ever has contact with. Third, courtesy and good oral communication skills are highly important.

Display a positive attitude and a pleasing personality, gain a few years of experience, and you may move up to a supervisory position. If you really want to make a long-term career in retail sales and want to become a middle or top manager, you probably need a college degree. Some college training coupled with retail experience may land you that executive position.

Regardless of your goal, you have to start somewhere, and selling in an all-night convenience, drug, or grocery store is a good start. Part-time jobs while you attend high school or college can give you a good idea about whether selling is for you. The customer service skills you learn will put you in a good position for those top-level jobs in your future.

Earnings

You may start out at minimum wage, but the median hourly wage in 2000 for retail store salespeople was $8.02, including sales commissions.

....

Printers

In a previous chapter, we talked about how reporters, writers, and editors worked though the night to be sure that our morning newspaper is delivered to our homes, put into those boxes on the corner, and distributed to stores and to the vendors on the street. Well, that was just part of the story. Printing press operators are also crucial to our morning reading pleasure.

These professionals prepare the presses by installing the printing plate, mixing solutions, fixing the pressure, applying ink, loading the paper, and making sure that the paper fits the press. After that, press operators have to monitor the operation, watching to see that the ink is evenly distributed and that the paper doesn't jam. If that happens, the press operator stops the press and makes adjustments.

Press operators may also have to maintain the presses and make minor repairs. Presses for major newspapers are large web presses that sometimes require several operators and some assistants. Large rolls of paper have to be fed into the presses, which then print on both sides of the paper at once.

The press also cuts the papers to size, assembles, and folds them. Some presses are now at least partially computerized. All of this work requires physical and mental alertness and an ability to fix things quickly.

The press room is usually noisy, and operators are generally on their feet almost all the time. There are printing presses everywhere, but job opportunities may be more plentiful in larger cities such as Chicago, New York, Los Angeles, and Washington, D.C.

What It Takes

If this night-owl career appeals to you, here's a look at what it takes to become a printing press operator. Because technology has entered this field as it has every other, taking courses in chemistry, electronics, color theory, and physics could boost your career opportunities. You will also have to be mechanically inclined, have good oral and written communication skills, and be mathematically proficient.

At any rate, when you start out, you will probably begin at the bottom of the ladder. After being assigned to loading and cleaning the presses, you may start to operate one-color presses and then move up to multicolor operations. It is a good idea to get as much experience on as many presses as possible as you learn your craft and build your career.

Apprenticeship is still available to beginners. It usually consists of on-the-job training under an experienced operator. Sometimes this training is supplemented by classroom instruction or correspondence courses. Any courses that you take in printing will benefit you, and it is important to keep updating your knowledge because of the ever-changing technological advances in the field.

Forecast and Earnings

If you have completed postsecondary training or qualify for apprenticeships, your job outlook is good. Even though many major U.S. newspapers have gone under, smaller papers are expected to increase in the coming years. The more experience you have, the more likely your chance of a good career in this business—especially if you are willing to work odd hours.

Commercial printers print offer another avenue for employment. They print everything from books to brochures and magazines, and most large printing operations run in shifts.

Median average hourly wages for newspaper printers in 2000 were $14.71. Commercial printers earned a median average wage of $14.91 per hour.

Adult Education Teachers

We have previously talked about professionals, such as doctors and nurses, whom we normally think of as working at night. There are, however, other professionals who also work irregular hours or split shifts and who might need a support staff to get them through the night. For example, teachers often work split shifts, evenings, and weekends. And we'll take a look at how these flexible shifts affect the work.

Adult education teachers often work two shifts, such as the morning and evening shift. Others just work weekends, and tutors work at any time that is convenient for their students, including evenings. In some cases, they work in an office, plant, or factory during the day and then teach at night. They may not be out on the streets saving lives, but they perform a vital service in every community.

These teachers instruct in a wide variety of basic and technical skills, including reading, writing, math, electronics, foreign languages, dance, photography, computer science, and cooking. These and other courses may prepare students for the General Educational Development (GED) examination, which is the high school equivalency test.

Many adult education teachers focus on a trade or craft that they make their living from, such as hairdressing. Others are certified to teach a specialized course, such as Japanese. In some cases, a bachelor's degree suffices for teaching adults; in others, a master's or doctorate is required. For some, a portfolio or samples of work is enough. Certification is necessary in some states.

Adult education teachers have to keep up with the latest in educational methods and their own fields by attending classes, seminars, and conferences. Some of this education is necessary to supplement a student's high school education; in other cases, it is an introduction to a much-needed job skill. In many cases, adult education teachers are involved in helping nonnative speakers learn the English language and the customs and culture of the United States.

For that reason, this country will continue to need adult education teachers in the near future. This is especially true for courses for the GED, job-enhancement skills, and learning English as a second language. You may advance to an administrative position or go into research, especially if you teach in a four-year college or university.

To be a teacher, you have to know your subject area thoroughly and be able to anticipate questions from your students. You must plan your lessons, spend time grading papers, and know how to explain the subject so that everyone understands it.

To be an effective teacher, you also need a passion for learning and an eagerness to pass on your knowledge to your students. In that way, you also learn from your students and begin to build a community with common goals and shared knowledge.

Earnings

Adult education teachers earned an average hourly rate of $16.12 in 2000. If you are self-employed or work part-time, you receive no benefits.

Qualifications for Night Owls

So, now that we have explored some possibilities for night-owl careers, you need to take a good look at yourself, your capabilities, your aptitudes, your interests, your knowledge, and your experience to see where you might fit in best.

In most cases, you have to be flexible, adaptable, reliable, and have a good sense of humor. In so many of these jobs, you deal directly with a wide variety of people, so your customer service, public relations, and communications skills have to be highly developed.

For some night-owl careers, you need to be sensitive to people's emotional and physical needs; for others, you are responsible for their safety, comfort, and security. Still others emphasize education and transmission of information. And, luckily, some are there to entertain and amuse us.

For all, however, you face the challenges of sleep deprivation, some eating irregularities, and a disrupted social life. But if you do what you love, these disadvantages won't matter. And besides, just remember—no rush hours!

....

For Further Information

For more information, contact the following organizations.

Graphic Arts Technical Foundation
200 Deer Run Road
Sewickley, PA 15143
www.gain.net

Graphic Communications Council
1899 Preston White Drive
Reston, VA 20191

Graphic Communications International Union
1900 L Street NW
Washington, DC 20036
www.gciu.org

The National Center for ESL Literacy Education
4646 Fortieth Street NW
Washington, DC 20016
www.cal.org/ncle

National Retail Federation
325 Seventh Street NW, Suite 1100
Washington, DC 20004
www.nrf.com

Printing Industries of America
100 Daingerfield Road
Alexandria, VA 22314
www.gain.net

Retail, Wholesale, and Department Store Union
30 East Twenty-Ninth Street, Fourth Floor
New York, NY 10016
www.rwdsu.org

The U.S. Department of Education
Office of Vocational and Adult Education
4090 MES
400 Maryland Avenue SW
Washington, DC 20202
www.ed.gov

Additional Resources

The American Correctional Association
4380 Forbes Boulevard
Lanham, MD 20706
www.corrections.com/aca

The American Institute of Graphic Arts
164 Fifth Avenue
New York, NY 10010
www.aiga.org

American Probation and Parole Association
c/o Council of State Governments
P.O. Box 11910
Lexington, KY 40578
www.appa-net.org

American Society of Magazine Editors
919 Third Avenue
New York, NY 10022
www.asme.magazine.org

American Society of Media Photographers
150 North Second Street
Philadelphia, PA 19106
www.asmp.org

American Society of Newspaper Editors
11690B Sunrise Valley Drive
Reston, VA 20191
www.asne.org

Association for Education in Journalism and Mass
   Communication
234 Outlet Pointe Boulevard, Suite A
Columbia, SC 29210
www.aejmc.org

CEGA Services
P.O. Box 81826
Lincoln, NE 68501

Communications Workers of America
501 Third Street NW
Washington, DC 20001
www.cwa-union.org

Council of Hotel and Restaurant Trainees
P.O. Box 2835
Westfield, NJ 07091

International Civil Aviation Organization
ICAO Public Information Office
999 University Street
Montreal, QU H3C SH7
Canada
www.icao.int

International Association of Fire Chiefs
4025 Fairridge Drive
Fairfax, VA 22033
www.iafc.org

International Union of Electronic, Electrical, Salaried,
  Machine, and Furniture Workers
1126 Sixteenth Street NW
Washington, DC 20036
www.iue-cwa.org

National Association of Schools of Dance
11250 Roger Bacon Drive, Suite 21
Reston, VA 20191
www.arts-accredit.org

National Cable and Telecommunications Association
1724 Massachusetts Avenue NW
Washington, DC 20036
www.ncta.com

National Railroad Construction and Maintenance Association
122 C Street NW, Suite 850
Washington, DC 20001
www.nrcma.org

Professional Photographers of America, Inc.
229 Peachtree Street NE, Suite 2200
Atlanta, GA 30303
www.ppa.com

Radio-Television News Directors Association
1000 Connecticut Avenue NW, Suite 615
Washington, DC 20036
www.rtnda.org

The Society of Illustrators
128 East Sixty-Third Street
New York, NY 10021
www.societyillustrators.org

The Society of Publication Designers
60 East Forty-Second Street, Suite 721
New York, NY 10165
www.spd.org

United States Telecom Association
1401 H Street NW, Suite 600
Washington, DC 20005
www.usta.org

About the Author

Louise Miller is something of a night owl herself since she has taught English on a split shift. She also understands what it means to burn the midnight oil by writing, editing, and researching as a freelancer. This night-owl spirit comes from her love of languages, especially English and German. She started out as a German teacher and teaches it today, after having studied in Vienna, Austria, and Bonn, Germany. She has taught German at the Universities of Kansas, Missouri, and Illinois.

Her love of English led her to teaching and publishing. She has taught English at community and business colleges, has conducted writing workshops, and has worked both full-time and freelance for various publishing houses. These include Compton's Encyclopedia, Rand McNally & Company, Marshall Cavendish, and World Book. Miller was also research coordinator for television quiz shows in Los Angeles, and she has written three other career books—two on careers for animal lovers and one for those who want to work with nature—and a children's book on Turkey.